# TO PRESERVE THESE RIGHTS

Kennikat Press

**National University Publications**

Multi-disciplinary Studies in the Law


*General Editor*

Rudolph J. Gerber
*Arizona State University*

Robert L. Spurrier, Jr.

# TO
# PRESERVE
# THESE RIGHTS

## Remedies for the Victims of Constitutional Deprivations

National University Publications
KENNIKAT PRESS     //     1977
Port Washington, N. Y.     //     London

.Copyright © 1977 by Kennikat Press Corp. All rights reserved. No part of this publication may be reproduced, stored in a retrieval system, or transmitted, in any form or by any means, electronic, mechanical, photocopying, recording, or otherwise, without the prior written permission of the publisher.

Manufactured in the United States of America

Published by
**Kennikat Press Corp.**
Port Washington, N. Y. / London

**Library of Congress Cataloging in Publication Data**

Spurrier, Robert L., Jr.
    To preserve these rights.

    (Kennikat Press multi-disciplinary studies in the law) (National university publications)
    Bibliography: p.
    Includes index.
    1. Civil rights—United States. 2. Remedies (Law)—United States. I. Title.
KF4749.S75        342'.73'0850269        77-7985
ISBN 0-8046-9199-1

*For My Students*
*with the prayer that they need never make use of the*
*remedies discussed in these pages*

# CONTENTS

# PREFACE

In the ringing words of the Declaration of Independence Thomas Jefferson asserted that men possess "certain unalienable rights" and that governments are instituted "to secure these rights." The natural-law basis for Jefferson's political philosophy may be questioned by many today, but few will argue with the proposition that individuals in the United States are endowed with basic civil liberties essential to individual freedom as we know it. Embodied in the Bill of Rights and elsewhere in the Constitution, these rights and liberties form the basis for our free society.

Unfortunately, government does not always operate to preserve these rights. In some instances the government's activities work to destroy the basic civil liberties of the individual. Such destruction may be the result of carelessness or the product of a deliberate effort, but the results are the same. The individual's rights are lessened and the promise of the American Revolution is dimmed when the power of organized society is used to destroy rather than to preserve these rights.

For nearly two centuries Americans have turned to the courts of law to secure protection of their legal rights. The courts have on occasion been hostile, at times seemed apathetic, and yet frequently acted responsively. The premise underlying this volume is that individuals must continue to have access to the judiciary in their efforts to secure their constitutional rights. The problem to be considered is how adequately the remedies for constitutional-rights deprivations fill the need to preserve these rights. Beyond this, suggestions are offered to strengthen the remedial system and to allow the individual more adequately to protect his rights against government interference.

Each of the four chapters dealing with presently available remedies (Chapters 2-5) begins with a series of hypothetical cases. These cases have proved useful as a teaching technique to focus attention on the problems of remedies and to crystallize opinions on remedial specifics. Any resemblance between fictitious characters and places in the hypothetical cases and real persons and places is, as the traditional disclaimer goes, purely coincidental. The hypotheticals should be read and considered before reading the rest of the chapter. Ideally, this will give the reader an opportunity to think out, on the basis of his own values, a personal approach to the remedial problem presented in the chapter. Then, in considering the remaining portion of the chapter, the reader can measure the present law against those individual values.

The proposals for reform which conclude the volume are not a cure-all. Indeed, as proposed reforms, their operation in practice has not been tested. They may be flawed to a serious degree. Still, if they provide the basis for a more serious consideration of the shortcomings of the remedies provided by American law for the victims of constitutional-rights deprivations, they will be well worth the effort expended in devising them.

Thanks go to C. Herman Pritchett, Stanley Anderson, and Thomas Schrock of the University of California, Santa Barbara, for their perceptive comments on the initial stages of this project, and to Harold Sare, chairman of the Department of Political Science at Oklahoma State University, for his encouragement and support during the completion of the manuscript. Finally, my appreciation goes to Kelly Murphy for her assistance with the final proofs and to my students who saw a good deal less of me than I would have liked during the final months of work on the manuscript and who understood the problems which accompany such an undertaking.

# TO PRESERVE THESE RIGHTS

# Chapter 1

# Constitutional Remedies:
# An Overview

> *The very essence of civil liberty certainly consists in the right of every individual to claim the protection of the laws, whenever he receives an injury.*
>
> —Chief Justice Marshall in Marbury v. Madison (1803)[1]

This work is an inquiry concerning legal remedies. It is an attempt to determine how adequately American law provides that protection deemed by Chief Justice Marshall to be "the very essence of civil liberty" in the content of a particularly important class of legal injuries—violation of the federal constitutional rights of the individual by state officials. The thesis to be presented is that neither federal nor state law (nor both taken in conjunction) provides an adequate remedy for the individual who falls victim to deprivation of those rights, privileges, or immunities secured by the Constitution of the United States against state action. In the course of developing this thesis the shortcomings of the presently available "remedies" will be considered, along with some of the underlying realities which have thwarted remedial efforts. The final step will be to propose a plan for reform which arguably would place the law of American constitutional remedies much closer to the goal set out 175 years ago by John Marshall.

Legal remedies may be said to serve several functions.[2] They may provide compensation to the victim of a legal wrong. A compensatory remedy frequently finds the court awarding the victim money damages which must be paid by the wrongdoer in an effort to make the victim "whole" again— or as nearly so as can be accomplished by an award of money. Remedies may offer specific relief. For example, if you contracted to buy a particular 1932 automobile for a given price and the seller then refused to deliver, you might ask the court for an order for specific performance—in other words, to force the seller to live up to his end of the bargain. This remedy would be most effective if you very much wanted that particular car and none other. If you did not necessarily want the car in question any longer, you might seek compensatory damages for breach of contract. Remedies may bring about restitution. Let's say that Daniel Dishonest made off with Fred Farmer's prize bull. Fred could go to court in a civil case to seek restitution—namely, the return of the bull. (Of course, Daniel might also wind up in court again on a criminal charge brought by the appropriate authorities.)

In addition to providing compensation, offering specific relief, and bringing about restitution, legal remedies may operate to punish and to prevent. In civil cases involving intentional wrongdoing or gross negligence, courts may award damages in amounts far above those necessary to compensate the victim for his losses. The purpose of the additional amount is to punish the wrongdoer and to make an example of him to others who might consider the same course of action. (This is the reason such awards are known as *punitive* or *exemplary* damages.) Of course, any legal judgment against the wrongdoer may operate to deter future misconduct on his part, and if the decision is publicized others may be deterred as well.

While legal remedies thus have several aspects, the central concern of this book will be with compensation. This concern arises from the operating premise that constitutional violations will continue to occur and that there will therefore be a continuing need to provide compensation to the victims. With the total of government employees constantly on the increase, the number of potential perpetrators of constitutional deprivations has reached proportions sufficient to make constitutional violations almost inevitable. Unless we are willing to assume that the millions of government officials who are clothed with the power of state or national government are incapable of errors of constitutional magnitude—or are to a man deterred from constitutional wrongs—there will be a continuing need for a remedy.

## THE SCOPE OF INQUIRY

This book does not attempt to deal with all violations of legal rights. Its coverage extends only to the level of federal constitutional rights and state governmental violations of those rights. The reason for this selectivity is both reasoned and practical. As a matter of practicality we cannot hope to deal with the entire breadth of legal remedies in a study of this length. As a matter of reasoned choice, constitutional rights present those rights highest on the legal scale. Federal constitutional rights are proclaimed by that document to be of the highest order. The supremacy clause in Article VI establishes the Constitution's position of legal pre-eminence over federal statutes and treaties as well as over state constitutions and laws.[3] Those rights declared by the Constitution to be of particular importance have been included by the action of the people in a process which transcends ordinary lawmaking. An extraordinary majority is necessary even to propose a right for inclusion in the Constitution, and an even larger majority is required for acceptance of the proposal. Once accepted, the right is placed beyond the reach of ordinary governmental activity. Only by the means of the same extraordinary process can the people of the United States lower one of their rights from its exalted position of inclusion in the Constitution.

The very possibility of such demotion, however, serves to point up an important characteristic of a constitutional right. It achieves its status in the American legal system because of its formal inclusion in the nation's fundamental charter—and only because of that inclusion. One may speak of permanent moral rights embodied in the Constitution, but there is no permanence guaranteed to constitutional embodiment. Ronald Dworkin has argued in the following terms:

If citizens have a moral right of free speech, then governments would do wrong to repeal the First Amendment that guarantees it, even if they were persuaded that the majority would be better off if speech were curtailed.[4]

Even granting Dworkin's premise that there is some unalienable moral right to free speech, it is obvious that repeal of the First Amendment is not impossible merely because that action would remove legal protection from the moral right, and, further, that, if such repeal were accomplished (even though arguably a moral wrong), the right of free speech would at that moment cease to be a federal constitutional right. Thus the rights which provide the setting for this study are not rights of guaranteed permanence; rather, they are those rights which currently are felt to deserve the highest legal status by a sufficiently large segment of society to secure their inclusion in the Constitution (or to prevent their removal). Whenever the people in their wisdom determine to remove the umbrella of constitutional protection from a given right, it ceases to be of interest in the remedial framework presented here; but so long as there are any constitutional rights, the remedial necessity remains.

Consideration of violations of federal constitutional rights might center on national-governmental action as well as on state action. Recent revelations of official wrongdoing surrounding the Watergate affair, the FBI, the IRS, and the CIA have reminded us all that national governmental power—like that of the states—is subject to abuse. It is at the state and local level, however, that the likelihood of abuse remains the greatest. There are more officials at these levels, the preponderance of law enforcement work continues to take place at these levels, and the education function (with its attendant risks of constitutional violations) is still largely a state and local responsibility; thus on a daily basis the "average citizen" is more likely to come into face-to-face contact with state and local officials than with the activity of federal officers. For these reasons we will concentrate primarily on remedies for federal constitutional violations at the state and local levels.

## THE JUDICIAL REMEDY AND ITS ALTERNATIVES

The remedies considered will be almost entirely judicial in nature, but it should at least be noted in passing that other methods for dealing with official misconduct are sometimes available to the victim of constitutional deprivation. In those states lacking a constitutional prohibition against private bills the legislature offers a route to redress (without, of course, an authoritative finding of the constitutional violation per se); some persons have sought and received relief by this approach. The shortcomings of the legislative claims-handling process are obvious, however, when considered in the light of the need for a continuous and impartial system for reaching determinations concerning compensation. There is first the appearance—no matter what the reality—of partisan political considerations entering the process. A private bill must have sponsorship by a member of the legislature, and his failure to introduce a bill could be seen by the public as a manifestation of partisan hostility toward a claimant who happened to be affiliated with the wrong political party.

The infrequency of legislative sessions in some of the less urbanized states means that a claimant, even if successful, may have to wait up to two years just to receive a hearing on his petition for relief; and even if he is heard, the bicameral legislative structure of forty-nine of our fifty states can mean that while one house is acting favorably the other is either not acting or acting negatively on the claim.

Further, state legislatures are not usually equipped to deal with such claims on a systematic basis. Even the Congress of the United States, which has a fairly well-developed system for handling claims, has been criticized for attempting to perform a function properly left in the hands of the judiciary, which is accustomed to handling individual cases for monetary relief.[5]

Finally, and perhaps most importantly, legislative relief is a matter of grace rather than legal right. The victim assumes the role of supplicant when he approaches the legislature for his relief. This is a far cry from being able "to claim the protection of the laws," as Marshall phrased it, when a constitutional deprivation has occurred. The victim should be legally entitled to appropriate relief rather than being left begging for legislative mercy.

Administrative mechanisms have also appeared from time to time in an effort to deal with the problem of official abuse of authority. Conspicuous examples are the so-called police review boards and the more recent ombudsman-like offices established to investigate individuals' complaints. Significantly, these agencies normally are empowered neither to rule on constitutional issues (the province of the judiciary, as noted above) nor to award money damages. They may in some instances be able, by publicity or official reprimand, to deter future abuses, but their function is not to provide compensation to the victim of a constitutional deprivation.

Some states, following the lead of the national government, have adopted tort claims acts which allow private parties to sue the state for certain legal wrongs committed by state officers. While these statutory provisions may in such instances allow the victim of a constitutional deprivation to sue the state (a sure source of recovery), they are not well suited to the remedial needs which confront us, for at least three reasons. First, most are patterned on the premise that the state shall be liable to the same extent and under the same rules as a private employer. Doctrinal problems arise immediately because a private employer, not being a governmental agency, cannot commit a constitutional violation through the actions of his employees. There simply is no state action without the state. Thus, the rules of private tort law are not adapted to constitutional violations.

A second problem is the exception to liability made by such acts for intentional torts. The state retains immunity from the doctrine of respondeat superior when its agent acted intentionally, and recovery is denied. Because many, if not most, constitutional deprivations are the result of intentional activity, the loophole engulfs the remedy.

Finally, the litigant (even if successful) must surrender a sizable portion of his award to his attorney in the form of legal fees. He is made "whole— less a percentage."

## THE SUPREME COURT AND CONSTITUTIONAL RIGHTS

A remedial system based on the authoritative determination of a constitutional deprivation must be centered on the judicial branch of government. Because we are here concerned with federal constitutional rights, the United States Supreme Court naturally attracts our attention in a most compelling fashion. As the historically sanctioned, albeit originally self-proclaimed,[6] illuminator of the fundamental text of American government, the Supreme Court is the ultimate judicial expositor of constitutional rights. We are therefore concerned with its pronouncements on the fundamental rights in question, and we are also concerned with its relationship to lower courts, state and federal, in our effort to determine the remedial effectiveness of current American law.

While the Supreme Court is the supreme authority on matters of constitutional interpretation, the political process does not give it carte blanche to define the relationships between the individual and the states. Lest we forget, aroused reaction in the states to Chisholm v. Georgia (1793) produced the first amendment to the Constitution subsequent to the adoption of the Bill of Rights in 1791.[7] Although the Court has fared better in recent years, the tribunal's "last word" carries no guarantee of permanence. A new combination of political forces may soon relegate the rule in question to a footnote in constitutional history either by the most obvious method, formal amendment (the most recent example being the Twenty-sixth Amendment in response to the Court's holding in Oregon v. Mitchell [1970] concerning the 18-year-old vote in state elections), or by a more subtle mode, such as changing the philosophy of the Court through the appointment process. One need only consider the fate of Plessy v. Ferguson (1896) or Hammer v. Dagenhart (1918) to see the point.[8] Nevertheless, so long as the Court's "last word" stands it provides the standard by which the rights of the individual are measured, and this caveat on the susceptibility of the law to change does nothing to detract from the importance of the Supreme Court as the enunciator of present constitutional meaning.

It is sometimes tempting to accept announced doctrine as accomplished fact. It is often reassuring to contemplate the well-turned phrases of a particularly fine opinion by a Black or a Harlan, but recent studies by political scientists, law students, and others should be sufficient to remind us that constitutional doctrine is not self-enforcing.[9] These "impact studies" attempt to measure empirically that which—on some issues—is all too obvious. Consider the rule of law on segregated educational facilities set down in Brown v. Board of Education (1954), and consider the results even today. Granting that significant progress has been made, especially in the South, it remains obvious that the rule announced by Chief Justice Warren was far from self-enforcing.

Given these warnings about the danger of overemphasis on the Supreme Court, it is well to consider the unique position of that institution in the American judicial system when it comes to federal constitutional rights.

The traditional textbook depicts two largely independent sets of courts, federal and state, connected by a line (from the state's court of last resort to the United States Supreme Court) that is labeled "appeal or certiorari." Considering the bewildering array of cases which arise in any given year in the state and federal courts this diagram has considerable merit, but in our more limited context of federal constitutional rights a somewhat different schematic may help clarify the importance of the Supreme Court.

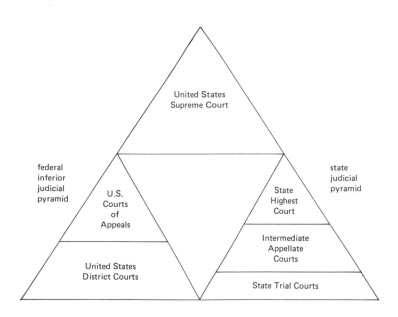

**FIGURE 1. United States Constitutional Interpretation Pyramid**

In Figure 1 the inferior federal courts and the state courts appear as almost entirely separate pyramids which support a third pyramid, the United States Supreme Court. Taken as a whole, these three form a larger, all-inclusive pyramid—the United States constitutional interpretation pyramid—with the Supreme Court at the apex. For the purposes of this study, this diagram is a convenient one in that it calls to mind three important facts: (1) On matters of federal constitutional interpretation, the Supreme Court occupies a preeminent position when it chooses to act. (2) The contact between the Supreme Court and the lower pyramids is not a continuous process on all fronts. (3) The implementation of the decisions rendered by the Supreme Court is often the responsibility of those who inhabit the lower slopes of the pyramid.

The ultimate authority of the Supreme Court in matters of federal constitutional interpretation is indicated by placing it atop the other pyramids. This positioning reminds us that when the Court accepts and decides a case its word literally is law.

The intermittent contact between the Supreme Court and lower courts comes about as a result of the Court's almost total control over its docket and of physical necessity. Being able to decide only slightly over one hundred cases a term with full opinion, the Supreme Court leaves most final decisions to the courts at the tops of the two inferior pyramids. For the parties in these cases, the United States Court of Appeals or the court of last resort in the state is the giver of the last word. This fact is symbolized in the diagram by the small areas of contact between the Supreme Court and the lower courts.

In the cases requiring further judicial action the parties must look to the lower courts even after winning a favorable decision from the United States Supreme Court. If we consider the citizen in his relation with the state to be at "ground level," it will be noted that his largest area of contact with the constitutional interpretation pyramid is at the trial court level. The diagram thus reminds us that the successful litigant most often receives his relief from the trial court.

The diagram, thus understood, should help us avoid the "upper court" myth while at the same time indicating that, so far as the authoritative interpretation of the individual's constitutional rights against the state is concerned, the Supreme Court has the option of pronouncing the judicial last word.[10]

## ATTRIBUTES OF AN ADEQUATE REMEDIAL SCHEME

We now turn to the standards by which the adequacy of a remedy is to be measured. Five elements are employed in this study. First, provision must be made for compensation of the victim, both for the constitutional deprivation per se and for any out-of-pocket expenses sustained as the result of the deprivation. Second, there must be a source of recovery sufficient to satisfy the amount of the award. Third, the remedy must, to the maximum degree feasible, remove the legal and extra-legal consequences of the deprivation. Fourth, the remedy must be available to all, regardless of social or financial status. Fifth, the remedy must provide for speedy determination of the issues and satisfaction of the judgment.

## PRESENTLY AVAILABLE "REMEDIES"

In the course of demonstrating the need for a more adequate remedial scheme to provide for redress of constitutional deprivations, four presently available "remedies" will be examined. The first will be civil actions brought by the victim against the offending officer as an individual, in either federal or state court. Our attention will then shift to the victim-plaintiff's attempts to secure compensation from the governmental entity that served as the source of authority under which the officer was acting. The third area of inquiry will concern the operation of the "exclusionary rule" made mandatory upon the states in criminal proceedings by Mapp v. Ohio (1961) and its progeny. Finally, the remedial aspects of the criminal law will be considered to determine its utility in securing redress for constitutional deprivations.

At the conclusion of the four separate evaluations an overall assessment of presently available remedies will be made to demonstrate that neither singly nor in conjunction do these legal devices adequately provide for the redress required under the standards set out above. Having reached this conclusion, the remaining task to be accomplished in the study will be the development of at least the basic outline of a more adequate remedy for the victims of deprivations of rights secured against state action by the Constitution of the United States.

# Chapter 2

# Suits Against the Officer:
# A Shallow Pocket Seldom Touched

We begin the examination of presently available remedies for constitutional deprivations with consideration of the traditional common law device for the redress of legal wrongs—money damages. Four hypothetical cases are presented at the outset to introduce the problem area of the chapter quickly and in nontechnical terms. The hypothetical cases also provide the reader with an opportunity to apply a personal sense of justice to "fact situations" which might give rise to litigation of the type discussed in this chapter.

### HYPOTHETICAL CASE 1

On the night before the general election in Credibility Gap, Kansas, it appeared that incumbent Sheriff Sammy Sidewinder was in for a tough reelection battle against his reformer opponent, Daniel Doright. About midnight, Deputy Sheriff Slim Witt decided to "help things along a bit" and, acting without a search warrant or an arrest warrant, he broke into Doright's home and arrested him for concealing stolen property. The morning newspaper, the Credibility Gap *Bridge*, carried the story of the arrest in an election day headline story; Doright lost the election by a vote of 1,200 to 1,190. Thus Sammy Sidewinder was elected to another four-year term, with an annual salary of $14,000. It was later determined that Deputy Witt's actions were unconstitutional and furthermore that he knew all along that the "concealing stolen property" allegations were completely untrue. In addition, repairs to Doright's door (kicked in by Witt) cost $55.19. If Doright sues Witt for consitutional-rights violations, should Witt have to pay? If so, how much?

## HYPOTHETICAL CASE 2

After the election scandal discussed in Case 1, there was continuing controversy in Credibility Gap. Ministers preached sermons about the abuse of governmental power, the *Bridge* ran editorials, and numerous discussions and debates took place around town. Supporters of Doright began wearing black armbands to symbolize their outrage, and several high school students wore the armbands into the civics class of Tommy Truant, the football coach and civics teacher, who demanded that they remove them immediately. When the students refused, Truant had them removed from his classroom (even though they claimed a constitutional right to silent, nondisruptive political protest) and refused to allow them to take any further examinations (so they received no credit for the semester in social science). Apparently Truant was unaware of the Supreme Court decision in Tinker v. Des Moines School District (1969), which held that students had the right to wear black armbands to class in protest against the Vietnam war. If one of the students sues Tommy Truant for constitutional-rights violations, should Truant have to pay? If so, how much?

## HYPOTHETICAL CASE 3

Thoroughly angered over the action of Tommy Truant, students and parents agreed to stage a protest march to the school board office in Credibility Gap to present a petition to the board demanding Truant's firing. They were aware, however, that they would need a parade permit for their march, so they went to the City Hall and asked for one from Nellie Nepotism, the city clerk. Nellie quickly conferred with her brother, the mayor, and returned to tell the parents and students that their request had been denied. Under the city charter, permits are to be granted "at the discretion of the city clerk." In his hurried conversation with Nellie, the mayor had threatened to fire her if she granted the permit. In a court test of the city charter provision concerning parade permits, a court later found it to be unconstitutional as a violation of the First and Fourteenth Amendments to the United States Constitution. If one of the would-be marchers sues Nellie, should she have to pay? If so, how much?

## HYPOTHETICAL CASE 4

Finally, in frustration, the citizens who were outraged by the election scandal, the school situation, and the mayor's action decided to attempt removal of Mayor Nepotism from office. Under the city charter of Credibility Gap, removal of a mayor is accomplished by first submitting a petition signed by 250 registered voters and then holding a special removal election. If the voters in the election vote to remove the mayor, the office is declared vacant and a new mayor is elected one month later. The charter also provides that the validity of the signatures on the petition shall be determined by the municipal judge and that there is no appeal from his decision.

The irate citizens quickly gathered 403 signatures on their petition and submitted them to Judge X. E. Cutioner, the municipal judge. After receiving the petition, the judge placed a phone call to Mayor Nepotism to tell him what was happening. Later that evening the mayor and the judge met for a private conference at a local restaurant. Subsequent meetings were held on three consecutive evenings. Then Judge Cutioner ruled that only 227 signatures were valid—which meant that the mayor would not have to face the special election. Although the petitioners were able to produce 397 registered voters willing to swear they had signed the petition, Judge Cutioner stood by his decision.

The following day the newspaper ran a headline story in which it was revealed that Judge Cutioner and Mayor Nepotism were secret partners in a business which had just received a lucrative contract from the city to conduct a public opinion survey on the need for city improvements. Both the judge and mayor received $1,000 payments from the business concern as "consultants," and their contract provided that they would receive additional payments of $250 per month for one year "so long as both hold office in the City of Credibility Gap." Assuming that Judge Cutioner's decision on the signatures was arbitrary and that the constitutional rights of the petitioners were violated by his decision, should he have to pay damages if one of the petitioners brought suit against him? If so, how much?

Our concern in this chapter is with the ability of the victim deprived of constitutional rights to sue the officer who brought about the violation. The chapter does not deal with all legal wrongs, of course, nor does it deal with all wrongdoers. Constitutional deprivations, as defined for this study, require state action, and only when that essential element is present can a legal wrong come within the scope of our inquiry. Such state action, however, does not come about in some mystical fashion behind swirling mists of smoke; it occurs when an individual, clothed with the power of the state, acts in a manner prohibited by the Constitution of the United States. Thus, for an individual to be the proper subject for consideration here, he must, first, be imbued with the authority of the state, and, second, he must have acted in violation of constitutional standards concerning state action. When these tests are met, it may be that civil liability in damages will follow.

Our federal form of government gives rise to the possibility of damages being available through two separate judicial systems, state and federal. In the pages that follow, consideration will be given to both levels of government in an effort to assess the utility of the damage remedy for constitutional deprivations.

In addition to dual judicial systems there may be dual sources of recovery. The individual officer is one source of money damages. The other is the employing entity, under whose authority the officer was acting at the time of the constitutional deprivation. Because of the substantial differences involved in proceeding against these two potential sources of recovery the present chapter will concentrate on individual-officer liability, and the following chapter will be concerned with securing damages against governmental entities.

## THE FEDERAL REMEDY

In our consideration of individual-officer liability we begin with the high road of federal law where, thanks to the Reconstruction Congress, we have a statute specifically designed for our purposes. Passed in the height of feeling against harassment of the newly freed Blacks by certain unreconstructed Southerners, particularly members of the Ku Klux Klan, the Fourth Civil Rights Act, 17 Stat. 13 (1871), has come, relatively free from change, to be included in the current federal law as 42 U.S.C. Section 1983:

Every person who, under color of any statute, ordinance, regulation, custom, or usage, of any State or Territory, subjects, or causes to be subjected, any citizen of the United States or other person within the jurisdiction thereof to the deprivation of any rights, privileges, or immunities secured by the Constitution and laws, shall be liable to the party injured in an action at law, suit in equity, or other proper proceeding for redress.

Although quite broad in its language, Section 1983 remained in the legal broom closet until the last decade, at least partially because of federal courts' reluctance to take its language at face value, accompanied by their generally careful pattern of noninterference with what they considered to be state problems.

Beginning with the case of Monroe v. Pape (1961), however, the Supreme Court breathed new life into the old statute by casting aside the self-imposed barriers to entertaining federal suits for damages under Section 1983. The case revealed allegations of shocking police impropriety.[1] Thirteen Chicago police officers were said to have invaded the Monroes' home in the early morning hours, forced them to stand naked in the living room while every room in the house was ransacked, and taken Mr. Monroe to the police station where he was-held incommunicado for ten hours while being interrogated about a murder which had taken place two days before. All of this was said to have taken place without the formality of a search warrant or an arrest warrant. Mr. Monroe finally was released without any charges having been filed against him.

There were two issues of key importance to suits against individuals[2] facing the Court in Monroe. The first concerned the meaning of "under color of" in the passage regarding state law. While there was an absence of precedent under Section 1983, similar language in criminal statutes passed by the Reconstruction Congress had received authoritative interpretation in two important cases, United States v. Classic (1941) and Screws v. United States (1944), which involved essentially the same issue.[3] Was the phrase "under color of" to be construed, narrowly, to mean only those abuses affirmatively sanctioned by the law of the state, or was it to be interpreted, broadly, to include all offenses committed by those who possessed the authority of the state whether or not their activities were in conformity with state law? Screws and Classic had opted for the broad view, Justice Douglas writing in the former that "It is clear that under 'color' of law means under 'pretense' of law." It is not surprising, then, to find Justice Douglas, also the author of the Court's opinion in Monroe, taking a similar stance with regard to the civil statute. "We conclude that the meaning given . . . was the correct one, and we adhere to it."

Concurring, Justices Harlan and Stewart found the historical record surrounding the enactment of Section 1983 less clear than did Justice Douglas, but they felt obliged to hold to the interpretation in Classic and Screws:

Were this case here as one of first impression, I would find the "under color of any statute" issue very close indeed. However, in Classic and Screws this Court considered a substantially identical statutory phrase to have a meaning which, unless we now retreat from it, requires that issue to go for the petitioner here.[4]

Their votes brought the majority to eight on this issue; only Justice Frankfurter dissented.

The other issue to be settled was whether the existence of state remedies should preclude federal relief. Again over the strident dissent of Justice Frankfurter, the majority declined to bow to the defendants' position concerning the respect for the imperatives of federalism:

It is no answer that the State has a law which if enforced would give relief. The federal remedy is supplementary to the State and the state remedy need not be first sought and refused before the federal one is invoked. Hence the fact that Illinois by its constitution and laws outlaws searches and seizures is no barrier to the present suit in the federal court.[5]

Subsequent cases in both the Supreme Court and inferior federal courts have dealt with the problem of what constitute "rights, privileges, or immunities secured by the Constitution," but that problem need not detain us here since our concern is aroused only after this threshold has been crossed. Suffice it to say that Section 1983 has been found broad enough to provide remedies for all manner of Fourteenth Amendment violations, including both the relatively simple problems of discriminatory classification under the equal protection clause and the ever-expanding array of Bill of Rights guarantees which have been made applicable to the states by the operation of the due process clause.[6]

Another problem of interpretation involved in Section 1983 which need not concern us at this point is the provision for equitable remedies. Although we will have occasion to mention one case involving an injunction in connection with the amount of damages awarded under Section 1983 in a subsequent portion of this chapter, most of the injunction cases are beyond the scope of the present inquiry. They involve judicial action to prevent future violations. Our concern, as we said, is with securing adequate remedies after the violation has taken place.

This leaves us with two important areas for consideration. The first involves the meaning of the words "every person" in the opening sentence of Section 1983. The second turns on an evaluation of damage awards handed down in the years following the landmark Monroe decision.

It may well seem that the language of Section 1983 could be no clearer concerning individual liability for deprivations of federal constitutional rights under color of state law. "Every person" would seem to mean just that. On the face of the statute, no one in official capacity should be able to escape the damage remedy—at least insofar as the legal requirements are concerned. The broad reach of Section 1983 so interpreted is well illustrated by Picking v. Pennsylvania Railroad Company (3d Cir. 1945), in which the plaintiffs Ida M. Picking and Guy W. Picking brought suit against the defendant railroad and twenty-three individual defendants, seeking compensatory and punitive damages in the amount of $1,120,050. The Pickings attempted to reach almost everyone who had the remotest connection with their being returned from Pennsylvania to New York to face certain misdemeanor charges. Named as defendants were Thomas E. Dewey, then the District Attorney of New York County; Herbert H. Lehman, then Governor of New York; Arthur H. James, then Governor of Pennsylvania; Judge Louis Costuma, a New York City judge; a justice of the peace in Pennsylvania identified only as Kieffer; and a cast of eighteen supporting players in the roles of jailers, agents, and officers—not to mention the railroad company itself. Although conceding that Mrs. Picking's complaint was ineptly drawn (she appeared as her own counsel) and that the issues were almost hopelessly muddled (for example, one Winger was alleged to have served a warrant improperly some twenty-nine days before Governor James was alleged to have signed it), the Court of Appeals reversed the trial court's dismissal of the case and ordered that Mrs. Picking be allowed to proceed against all of the defendants.

Having denied certiorari in Picking, the Supreme Court waited six years before it took up the question of whether Section 1983 had abrogated the common law immunities enjoyed by certain state officers in damage actions. Tenney v. Brandhove (1951) provided the vehicle for that task. The issue in the case was whether state legislators acting as such in their traditional sphere of activity were subject to Section 1983 liability, and the Court, speaking through Justice Frankfurter, held that they were not. Noting that both the Constitution of the United States and the constitutions of the states make specific provision for legislative immunity from suit in some circumstances, Frankfurter expressed doubt that Congress could abolish the legislators' immunity altogether, but he based his ruling on the narrower ground of congressional intent: "We cannot believe that Congress—itself a staunch advocate of legislative freedom—would impinge upon a tradition so well grounded in history and reason by covert inclusion in the general language before us."[7] Only Justice Douglas dissented. He argued that the Court was giving total immunity to state legislators even when their activities pervert legal forms for illegal ends. It was precisely this sort of problem that the statute contemplated, according to Douglas' reading of the congressional intent.

What the Court did for legislators in Tenney it was only too happy to do for its comrades-in-arms on the state bench in Pierson v. Ray (1967), a case that had its origins in the civil rights activism of that period in the South. The fifteen plaintiffs in the case were ministers whose attempt to use segregated bus facilities (a waiting room) led to their arrest under a state statute for posing a threat of breach of the peace and for failure to move on when ordered to do so. The ministers waived a jury trial, and the defendant Spencer, a municipal police justice in the state action, convicted and sentenced them. On appeal, one of the defendants (the plaintiffs in the Section 1983 action) was accorded a trial de novo and was acquitted by directed verdict. The charges against the other ministers were then dropped. The fifteen plaintiffs subsequently brought suit in federal district court under Section 1983. In that trial the jury found for the defendant judge and police officers. On appeal, the Fifth Circuit held Judge Spencer immune from Section 1983 liability but found the officers subject to civil liability under the statute even if they had been acting in good faith to enforce a law which had not yet been ruled unconstitutional.

On the issue of judicial immunity, the Supreme Court upheld the common law immunity extended by the Fifth Circuit:

Few doctrines are more solidly established at common law than the immunity of judges from liability for damages for acts committed within their judicial jurisdiction. . . .

. . . . . . . . . . . . . . . . . . . .

We do not believe this settled principle of law was abolished by [section] 1983, which makes liable "every person. . . ." The legislative record gives no clear indication that Congress meant to abolish wholesale all common-law immunities.[8]

So wrote Chief Justice Warren, certainly no foe of civil liberties.

Justice Douglas continued his one-man crusade for statutory literalism in Pierson, asserting once again that Tenney had been wrongly decided. Pointing to the debates surrounding the passage of what is now Section 1983, Douglas urged that the drafters knew full well that judges could be involved in the suppression of the rights of the newly emancipated Negroes and that they meant to fashion a remedy which would reach all those involved in the deprivations. To Douglas, "every person" still meant every person.[9]

The common law immunity preserved for judges by Pierson has more recently been extended to state prosecutors in Imbler v. Pachtman (1976), a case in which the plaintiff alleged that a California deputy district attorney knowingly used false testimony and suppressed material evidence in a criminal case which sent him to the state penitentiary. Such deliberate perversions of the adversary system, if proved, would clearly constitute a denial of constitutional due process under Napue v. Illinois (1959) and Brady v. Maryland (1963). Speaking for the five-man majority, Justice Powell opted for preservation of the common law's absolute immunity of prosecutors acting within the scope of their traditional duties (initiating prosecutions and presenting the state's case). He did so on the grounds that potential civil liability could deflect the prosecutor's energies from his public duties and make him timid in the execution of those duties. Further, if such fear of liability led a prosecutor to be overly cautious in presenting evidence to the jury, "the triers of fact in criminal cases often would be denied relevant evidence."

The majority in Imbler was fully aware that its decision concerning prosecutors might leave a constitutional-rights deprivation victim without a remedy. In its opinion, however, the price was worth paying:

To be sure, this immunity does leave the genuinely wronged defendant without civil redress against a prosecutor whose malicious or dishonest action deprives him of liberty. But the alternative of qualifying a prosecutor's immunity would disserve the broader public interest.[10]

The only potential solace offered was a reference to 18 U.S.C. Section 242, which provides for criminal penalties for such deprivations (an illusory threat at best; see Chapter 5), and to the hope of professional discipline of such devious prosecutors by their colleagues in the legal profession.

This time there was no one left to carry the banner of statutory literalism. The three remaining Justices (Justice Stevens did not participate) were willing to accept absolute immunity on the perjured testimony side of the coin, but they argued that liability should attach for unconstitutional withholding of material evidence.

Returning to the Pierson decision of 1967, we begin an examination of the rather clouded area of liability of police officers and other executive branch personnel under Section 1983. In Pierson, police officers received a measure of relief from the stringent language of the section. Although Chief Justice Warren found the issue not to be free from doubt, he reversed the Fifth Circuit on the issue of good faith enforcement of a statute later found to be unconstitutional:

We hold that the defense of good faith and probable cause, which the Court of Appeals found available to the officers in the common-law action for false arrest and imprisonment, is also available to them in the action under [section] 1983.

. . . . . . . . . . . . . . . . . .

We agree that a police officer is not charged with predicting the future course of constitutional law.[11]

Thus police officers—and, by implication, other state executive officers—acting in good faith under an apparently valid statute appeared to be free from Section 1983 liability. Their lot was not so happy as that of the legislator or the judge who escaped trial altogether, but it was at least better than their fate under the Fifth Circuit's interpretation of Monroe v. Pape.

The Court's subsequent decisions in Scheuer v. Rhodes (1974) and Wood v. Strickland (1975) apparently have undermined the strength of the good faith defense, at least to a degree. Scheuer arose out of the deaths of Kent State University students at the hands of the Ohio National Guard. In Section 1983 actions brought against Governor Rhodes, the Adjutant General and an assistant, various National Guard personnel, and the president of the university, the trial court dismissed the suits without requiring the defendants to respond to the plaintiffs' complaints. The dismissal was based on the theory that the cases were in actuality suits against the state (and hence barred by the Eleventh Amendment) or, in the alternative, that the defendants were absolutely protected by the common law doctrine of executive immunity.

On this meager record, the Supreme Court reversed. The controlling statement in Chief Justice Burger's opinion recognized that the breadth of an executive officer's duties must have an impact on his legal liability and so must the time frame in which the officer is forced to operate:

These considerations suggest that, in varying scope, a qualified immunity is available to officers of the executive branch of Government, the variation dependent upon the scope of discretion and responsibilities of the office and all the circumstances as they reasonably appeared at the time of the action on which liability is sought to be based. It is the existence of reasonable grounds for belief formed at the time and in light of all the circumstances, coupled with a good faith belief, that affords basis for qualified immunity of executive officers for acts performed in the course of official conduct.[12]

Wood v. Strickland (1975) indicates that liability standards may well be somewhat stricter. In that case, high school students were expelled for allegedly "spiking" the punch at a school party. The students sued, and the Supreme Court once again faced the issue of establishing the proper standard for the imposition of Section 1983 liability. This time the result was a more qualified good faith defense:

Therefore, in the specific context of school discipline, we hold that a school board member is not immune from liability . . . if he knew or reasonably should have known that the action he took within his sphere of official responsibility would violate the constitutional rights of the student affected, or if he took the action with the malicious intention to cause a deprivation of constitutional rights or other injury to the student.[13]

Under this test a claim of "ignorance of the Constitution" will not be adequate as a defense to a Section 1983 suit if the court determines that the defendant should have known about the constitutional rights involved. This in turn means that a defendant may be found liable even though he acted in good faith (but was not sufficiently aware of the rights of his victim). At least in the case of obvious wrongs, then, the Wood case opens the door to recovery, at least to a limited degree.

On the other hand, the cases discussed so far show that certain constitutional deprivations will go unremedied under Section 1983. The victim of a constitutional deprivation committed by a state legislator, judge, or prosecutor acting within the traditional limits of his duties will go uncompensated. The victim of the well-meaning policeman or other state official of the lower ranks of the state executive may also find his cupboard bare at the end of Section 1983 litigation if the officer acted in reasonable good faith. Whether the reasoning supporting these immunities and defenses is well founded or not, the fact remains that when they apply there is no Section 1983 remedy—at least from the perspective of money damages recovered from the individual who committed the constitutional-rights deprivation.

Passing from these leaks in the remedial umbrella provided by Section 1983, we may turn our attention to those situations in which recovery is possible. Although there is a division of lower court authority, the recent trend seems to be toward allowing damages for all deprivations instead of requiring "shocking" or "outrageous" conduct on the part of the officer. This fact, taken in conjunction with the realization that at least a sizable portion of the instances of constitutional-rights deprivations falls outside the immunities and defenses just discussed, opens at least the potential of a widely available remedy.

Unfortunately, an examination of recent decisions tends strongly to suggest that the potential has yet to be converted into actuality. While there are increasingly frequent reported cases involving successful Section 1983 litigation,[14] there are sufficient pitfalls to prevent meaningful recovery for many victims. The brief discussion of lower federal court decisions which follows is intended to illustrate some of these pitfalls.

In the case of a plaintiff who suffered an unconstitutional deprivation of liberty (false arrest and imprisonment), a jury in Champaign, Illinois, returned a verdict for the plaintiff and an award of $0.00. This award is patently absurd. In reaching this decision the jury found a constitutional violation and then concluded that the rights involved were worth absolutely nothing. By returning this verdict it demonstrated complete insensitivity to the entire problem that confronts us in this study. By allowing the judgment to stand on appeal, Joseph v. Rowlen (7th Cir. 1970), the Seventh Circuit displayed incredible judicial obtuseness. The value of a constitutional right has been reduced to absolute zero. Such verdicts cannot help but have a chilling effect on Section 1983 litigation.

The Third Circuit upheld a district court decision which found a constitutional violation but declined to award damages,[15] and the U.S. District Court for the Northern District of Ohio concluded that a high school student's constitutional right to due process before being expelled from high school because of the length of his hair was worth precisely one cent. As the trial judge put it:

There is no showing that the plaintiff has suffered any actual pecuniary loss or damage whatsoever. Indeed, it does not appear that he has even been annoyed or humiliated beyond what is usual in the course of a child's growth, and may, in fact, have been made a hero by some.[16]

From the last three cases discussed (all decided in recent years), it is clear that even successful plaintiffs under Section 1983 may come away without an award of damages in any way compensatory for the violation of their constitutional rights. It is likewise clear that should this style of judgment become widespread the incentive to sue (and to serve as counsel in such actions) will diminish nearly to the vanishing point.

Not all federal courts condone such chicanery, however. The Fifth Circuit recently sent a case back to the trial court with the following language:

Perhaps in some circumstances [only nominal damages] are all a man's freedom is worth, but though the price tag be a bargain, freedom is never valueless. A jury finding that a man's freedom is worthless is clearly erroneous. It is an impossible judgment to render against a sentient person, be he one legged, unschooled, and friendless or without earning capacity.[17]

At least in the Fifth Circuit we find recognition that constitutional rights, in and of themselves, are things of value. Whether or not the victim has been deprived of property, he has suffered a loss—and Section 1983 was designed to compensate that loss.

Other lower court decisions in the recent past illustrate additional possibilities—and drawbacks—of litigation under Section 1983. Gaston v. Gibson (E.D. Tenn. 1969) serves to illustrate the potential for recovering punitive as well as compensatory damages. The facts of the case involved "police brutality" against a 17-year-old University of Tennessee student who had gone to a hospital to determine the condition of some of his colleagues who had just been involved in an automobile accident. He was struck in the mouth by a constable described by the court as a "corpulent man of about six feet, two inches and weighing between 220 and 240 pounds."[18] As a result of the blow, the plaintiff's head struck the floor, causing an injury which brought on persistent headaches. His medical bills ran to $736.60. Compensatory damages were assessed in the amount of $10,000. The remainder of the $40,000 judgment was in the form of punitive damages.

Davidson v. Dixon (D. Del. 1974) serves as an object lesson to those who feel that state penitentiary inmates have no constitutional rights. The trial court found that the prisoner-plaintiff had been beaten by guards and that a superior officer was present and acquiesced. Finding a constitutional violation, the court awarded $1,500 in compensatory damages with joint and several liability of the guard-defendant and the superior-officer-defendant. In addition, $500 in punitive damages were assessed against each of the defendants. On appeal, the Third Circuit affirmed the judgment without opinion.[19]

These cases raise at least some hope for an optimistic assessment of what Section 1983 could become, but overall evaluation of the remedy must remain guarded. In these cases, as well as in others in which at least some award has been forthcoming, there remains to be considered the very serious problem of collecting the judgment after winning the suit.

State officials are not among the most regally rewarded laborers in the American vineyard, and those particular officers who frequently become embroiled in problems fraught with constitutional consequences—the police—are among the lowest of the low when it comes to financial rewards.[20] With such persons in the role of defendant the judgment will amount to little more than the paper on which it is written, and the plaintiff might be forgiven for saying what Lincoln is supposed to have attributed to the man who was about to be ridden out of town on a rail, "If it weren't for the honor of the thing, I'd just as soon walk." One can only speculate on the chances of plaintiffs like the 14-year-old boy in Roberts v. Williams (N.D. Miss. 1969) who was awarded $85,000 against a Negro trusty and a county prison farm superintendent in Mississippi.

The cases in which sizable monetary judgments have been secured in favor of the plaintiff are interesting from another perspective. In the large majority of instances, the awards have been calculated on ordinary tort grounds, with little or no consideration of the constitutional deprivation which brought them under federal jurisdiction in the first place.[21] Medical bills were tallied, lost wages were counted, pain and suffering were permitted to inflate the judgment beyond out-of-pocket losses, and of course punitive damages were allowed in appropriate cases, but the constitutional deprivation itself seldom has entered into the accounting process. It is as though the violation serves as a jurisdictional springboard and is then shunted aside.[22] The result is that, in most cases, the federal courts are acting as glorified state civil courts in tort actions for false imprisonment and the like without protecting the federal rights covered by Section 1983. In its own way, this method of calculating damages comes to much the same end as the $0.00 judgment. It, too, seems to say (albeit more subtly) that constitutional violations per se are not worth much in monetary terms.

Before passing to the consideration of remedies at the state level, it might be well to summarize what has been said thus far concerning the possibility of securing money damages for constitutional violations from state officials under 42 U.S.C. Section 1983. First, the "under color of law" language has been given broad scope, so that action need not be affirmatively sanctioned by state law to be within the reach of the statute. Second, the existence of separate state remedies does not bar the federal action. Third, state legislators, judges, and prosecutors enjoy complete immunity from suit under Section 1983 if their actions were taken in their official capacity, thus opening a gap in the statute's coverage. Fourth, this gap is widened by "good faith" defenses available to executive officers acting under what appears to be a valid state law. Fifth, even when a defendant can be found who is subject to liability under the statute, the number of cases in which damages have been awarded is quite small. Sixth, courts are still allowed to return judgments awarding one cent or even "zero." Seventh, even though there have been a few recent cases with sizable judgments under Section 1983, there is serious doubt as to the collectability of such judgments when the pocket into which the successful plaintiff must reach is that of a low-paid state employee. Finally, in any event little attention has been paid to constitutional violations per se when federal courts have calculated damages.

## STATE TORT REMEDIES

Having surveyed the high road of federal law and found chances for meaningful recovery limited, the prospective victim-plaintiff may consider the low road of state civil actions for damages. As he begins his quest for money damages under state law the victim ordinarily must proceed along a path marked out by the traditional common law forms of action in tort, as modified by local statute. These remedial formulae, having come down to us from English origins which long antedate the Constitution, are not specifically fashioned to provide compensatory relief for violations of federal constitutional rights. Rather, as a matter of coincidence, certain constitutional violations arise out of situations which were the concern of the judges who developed the early English principles concerning conduct among private individuals. Among the tort actions which have obvious relevance in the constitutional deprivation area are trespass (unreasonable searches and seizures), assault and battery (infliction of summary punishment without due process of law), false arrest, and false imprisonment (the latter two being compatible with a remedy for deprivation of liberty without due process of law). The issue confronting us is that of how successful our victim-plaintiff is likely to be as he proceeds along this path, marked by its ancient sign posts, in his search for compensation.

The next few pages could be devoted to a lengthy treatment of the complexities of the remedies just mentioned as to pleading, immunities, defenses, statutes of limitations, and the like, but they will not be. Such an undertaking, even supposing it had not taken place elsewhere,[23] would be pointless here because the state tort remedy for official abuse of constitutional rights amounts to little more than illusion. Such suits are seldom brought and less frequently won. Caleb Foote's 1955 article[24] remains the most frequently cited source on the issue of realistically available tort remedies for violation of individual rights, and the reasons for his dismal prognosis remain largely unchanged.

As an illustration of the problem, we may use the Fourth Amendment's guarantee of freedom from unreasonable searches and seizures, made applicable to the states through the due process clause of the Fourteenth Amendment in Wolf v. Colorado (1949), and the utility of the state tort action in trespass which corresponds, at common law, to the Fourth Amendment deprivation. The trespass action has been described as "completely impotent," primarily because damages normally are limited to out-of-pocket losses.[25] Because most unreasonable searches and seizures do not involve sufficient physical damage to the premises to form the basis for a substantial recovery, the trespass action has been rendered a practical nullity.[26]

False imprisonment and false arrest actions, on the other hand, do give rise to the possibility of larger awards for "pain and suffering," damage to reputation, humiliation, and the like. The inflated amount of potential damages, in contrast with that possible in a trespass action, has kept up what Foote described as "a steady trickle" of reported cases, yet even here the chances for recovery seem slim at best.

Factors militating against the victim's success are both legal and practical. First, there is the problem of the judgment-proof defendant. Second, there is the problem of the evidence that goes to the jury, which lowers the victim-plaintiff's "moral status" in their eyes. Third, there is the discretion as to the amount of damages to be awarded.

As noted in the preceding section on 42 U. S. C. Section 1983, the officer-defendant is likely to be possessed of a most shallow pocket, and the simple movement from federal to state jurisdiction will not increase his resources. Of course, the case of the uncollectable defendant is not new in state civil litigation, nor is the lawyer's advice to forget the idea of a suit.

Let us assume, however, that our victim has the "good fortune" to be deprived of his federal constitutional rights by a state officer with reachable resources, thus making him an attractive potential defendant,[27] and let us also assume that none of the common law immunities attach. What are the other factors which make the tort remedy so impractical?

If the plaintiff's claim is one with low "moral aspects," his chances of recovery remain minimal, and all too frequently this description will fit the victim of a constitutional deprivation:

> Very few of them are persons who are respectable in the sense that they have some measure of status and financial security in society and have acquired the kind of reputation which will be "damaged" by illegal police activity. Most police action operates at lower levels of society and the great majority of persons who are subjected to illegal arrests or searches and who are therefore potential tort plaintiffs come from the lowest economic levels, or minority groups, or are criminals or suspected of criminality. For such people, "the rules . . . are little more than mere pretensions."
>
> . . . . . . . . . . . . . . . . . . .
>
> The "moral aspects" of the cases of these potential plaintiffs ruin their chances of success in court. They lack the minimum elements of respectability which must be present to form a base upon which the fiction of reparation can operate.[28]

The "fiction of reparation" refers to the allowance for damage to reputation, for pain and suffering, and for humiliation, which makes the false arrest or false imprisonment action potentially rewarding even when monetary losses are small or nonexistent. This seemingly bright promise, however, carries with it the seeds of despair because to show such "damage," the reputation and position of the plaintiff must be paraded before the jury. This having been done, his social status and lack of socially approved "moral status" have also been fully revealed. When it appears that the plaintiff's reputation was sullied to begin with, the jury may simple conclude that the deprivation could have done nothing to lower it further, hence no damages should be forthcoming on this count. The amount likely to be awarded consequently recedes to near the zero point.

The lack of "moral status" can come before the jury in various ways, including testimony to impeach the credibility of the plaintiff's testimony and evidence on his lack of good reputation to mitigate damages. If the plaintiff happens to be notorious for his activities, the jury might well have assessed his "moral worth" without the benefit of such evidentiary devices. Imagine the chances of Charles Manson in a civil action for false arrest tried in a Los Angeles civil court after the glare of nationwide publicity he received in the Sharon Tate murder case. Even a change of venue seems unlikely to save a potential plaintiff in this situation.

Finally, on the "practical" side of tort actions is the jury's discretion over the measure of damages. As already noted in the description of the federal remedy, the spectacle of the award of damages in the amount of one cent is still to be found in American law.

One legal barrier not mentioned in the federal civil rights act discussion or noted above deserves passing mention. Statutes of limitations can make recovery against an officer impossible in those states adhering to the doctrine of civil death for persons in state prisons or jails. Being unable to sue while he is incarcerated, the victim of a constitutional deprivation might eagerly await his release date and subsequent day in court only to find that the statute of limitations for common law tort actions had long since tolled.[29]

This, in capsule form, is an assessment of the likely fate of the traveler on the path to recovery of money damages against an individual officer in the state courts. His chances of substantial recovery range from poor to none. For reasons both legal and practical, the state damage action remains largely illusory.[30]

It seems, then, at the conclusion of this brief survey of potential money damage remedies against individual state officers for deprivations of federal constitutional rights, that neither the state tort remedy nor the federal Section 1983 remedy provides an adequate avenue for redress. Returning to the hypothetical cases with which this chapter began, Deputy Sheriff Slim Witt is the most likely individual to be forced to pay damages. He can raise no "good faith" defense because he acted maliciously and intentionally, but the collection problem remains. Even if a court were to assess "constitutional damages," a deputy sheriff may well be judgment proof in all practical terms. Tommy Truant, the high school teacher, probably would be liable under Section 1983, although state tort liability seems less likely. The question would turn on whether he "should have known" about the right of the students to wear armbands in a nondisruptive protest. Two problems arise here. First, the problem of collectability is present. Second, the trial judge (if he is of the persuasion to minimize students' rights) could rule that Truant is not responsible for understanding the Supreme Court's ruling in the Tinker case. Nellie Nepotism, likewise a poor choice for collection of a sizable judgment, presents a sympathetic case for a jury. Threatened with the loss of her job, she complied with the mayor's orders. Additionally, she acted under a city charter provision which had not been declared unconstitutional at the time. This fact might be sufficient to place her in the realm of "qualified good faith immunity." Finally, Judge Cutioner is completely immune from suit. With the preservation of common law immunity at both the state and federal level as the rule, his victims simply have no remedy in damages.

The hypothetical cases illustrate the problem discussed throughout this chapter. While in some instances Section 1983 cases (and the state tort remedies) may provide a salutary beginning, they do little more than that. In sum, we may say that, for the victim-plaintiff, the individual state officer-defendant has a shallow pocket, seldom touched.

# Chapter 3

# Suits Against the Government: In Search of a Deeper Pocket

Three more hypothetical cases are presented for your consideration as you begin this chapter. In these cases, however, we are not concerned with the liability of the individual state officer. Instead, consider whether the governmental unit which employs the officer should have to pay money damages to compensate the victim of the constitutional-rights deprivation.

### HYPOTHETICAL CASE 5

While driving through Mudslide Flats, Mississippi, Henry "Homer" Hanks (a famous major league baseball player) experienced an automotive breakdown about 4:30 in the afternoon. Because he was a black man, none of the hamlet's three auto mechanics were willing to work on the car. (Mudslide Flats has no black population.) Unable to find a room in town, Hanks was forced to sleep in the back seat of his car that night. About midnight a group of unsavory citizens was gathering at the local cafe for their nightly meeting when Roger Redneck, the town constable, joined the party. He suggested "a little welcome party" for Hanks, and the group joined in suggesting ways to make it a "warm welcome." The cafe owner, fearing trouble, called the mayor—who quickly drove to the cafe in an attempt to stop the "welcome" before it began. Calling Roger Redneck aside, he told him to quit arousing the crowd and to prevent any attempts to harass Hanks. Redneck reluctantly agreed, and the mayor went home to bed. As soon as he left, Redneck and his cohorts resumed their planning. The result was a torchlight parade to Hanks' disabled vehicle. Hanks refused to come out of the car until Redneck appeared outside the window, wearing his uniform and badge, and ordered him out of the car. The crowd then set fire to the automobile (worth $8,000) and chased Hanks out of town. The next morning the mayor fired Redneck for his participation in the activity. Should the town have to pay damages, and if so, in what amount?

## HYPOTHETICAL CASE 6

During the annual New Year's Eve celebration in Partyville, Pennsylvania, Patricia Patrician had a bit too much to drink. She and her dinner companion, Conrad Commoner, decided to drive to her home rather than continue with the city-sponsored festivities. With Patricia driving her new sports car, the couple headed south on the main street of the town, narrowly missing several persons taking part in the celebration. Patricia then ran a red light, exceeded the speed limit, and ran a stop sign. Patrick Patrolman observed the violations and began pursuit in his police car. After a five-mile chase he finally managed to force Patricia to stop. She got out of the car, and then she attempted to slap Patrolman's face. (The idea that a mere policeman would dare stop the car of a Patrician—the town's wealthiest family—was more than she could comprehend.) Patrick grabbed her hand and attached his handcuffs—whereupon Conrad Commoner (from an average family in town) attempted to free Patricia by hitting Patrick with a beer bottle. The officer then lost his temper and used his nightstick to subdue Commoner with a blow to the nose. Turning to Patricia, he struck her on the arm with the nightstick as a "warning not to try anything." A doctor's examination in the police station determined that Commoner received a skull fracture in the incident, and Patricia Patrician was the recipient of a broken arm. If both Patricia and Conrad brought suits against the city of Partyville for damages, should either of them win? If so, how much?

## HYPOTHETICAL CASE 7

At the monthly staff meeting Marsha Metermaid had been reminded (for the two-hundredth time, it seemed to her) that her job was to give tickets to all cars parked in violation of city ordinances. The city of Arrowhead, Arizona, had a city ordinance which prohibited the parking of foreign cars in the city limits. It also had an ordinance which required the impounding of foreign vehicles receiving parking tickets. Shortly after leaving the staff meeting, Marsha spotted a Datsun pickup truck parked near the emergency entrance of the hospital. She wrote out a ticket and called for the tow truck. The owner of the truck (who was also its driver), Donald Doctor, had been called to the hospital from New Mexico to consult on the case of a patient with a strange illness which had defied diagnosis by local physicians. Needless to say, Dr. Doctor was angry to find his truck gone when he emerged from the hospital. Assuming the city ordinance is unconstitutional (arbitrary and capricious), should the doctor win damages in a suit against the city? If so, how much should the city be required to pay?

The victim of a violation of constitutional rights at the hands of a state officer may sue and recover money damages from the governmental entity, the officer, or not at all. The examination of the law and practical realities surrounding suits against individual officers in Chapter 2 led to the conclusion that the two latter possibilities are frequently identical. If, therefore, the victim-plaintiff is to secure more than a worthless judgment, the public treasury must be tapped.

Standing directly between the deserving plaintiff and his goal is the barrier of sovereign immunity, often capsulized in the maxim "The King can do no wrong." In some states the barrier has been lowered in recent years, but many plaintiffs find their chances for recovery as minimal as those of a British subject during the height of the monarchy.[1] How this doctrine, which originated as a restraint on the monarchy, has come to its present form and practice in American law is one matter to be dealt with later in this chapter. Our first task is to trace the English historical antecedents of the present-day American doctrine. Second, we will discuss the transplanting of the doctrine to American soil and the justifications which have been advanced for its continuation. Our attention will then shift to limitations on the scope of the doctrine which have evolved over the past two centuries in the United States. Finally, an attempt will be made to estimate the chances of the constitutional rights victim-plaintiff in the present (confused) state of the American law of governmental immunity.

## HISTORICAL BACKGROUND OF SOVEREIGN IMMUNITY

Although some legal scholars have attempted to trace the sovereign immunity concept to Roman origins,[2] others have denied such connections.[3] More recent writing leaves the question of possible ancient origins unsettled.[4] Our concern with the doctrine of sovereign immunity takes us to the common law of England, the direct ancestor of much American state law (either by judicial acceptance or by specific constitutional or legislative adoption), where it came to be a mixim that "The King can do no wrong."

A legal maxim, at least in theory, is a statement of "a principle of law universally admitted,"[5] but the particular maxim in question managed to undergo an interesting metamorphosis through the centuries in England. By the sixteenth century, the "modern" interpretation of the maxim had taken hold. Blackstone could write that in the eyes of the law, the king "is not only incapable of doing wrong, but even of *thinking* wrong: he can never mean to do an improper thing: in him is no folly or weakness."[6] This view of the perfect monarch is a far cry from the interpretation placed upon the maxim in the Middle Ages. Bracton's view was that the maxim meant that the king was *privileged* to do no wrong—that he was bound by the law.[7] Remedies against the king might have been weak necessarily, but in theory at least he was bound by the law—with a final appeal to the Pope in Rome as a possibility, which for a time in English history was more than an idle threat.[8]

Blackstone offers a "noble lie" thesis to explain and justify the "modern" view in his treatment of the royal prerogative. At the outset he states that, although the philosophical man will recognize that the king is merely "one man appointed by mutual consent to preside over many," he will nonetheless render the king the respect that the needs of society require; but for the masses this will not do. They soon will become restless if the notion is spread about the king is no better than they. For the purpose of maintaining social order, the law employs a fiction to keep these subjects of the realm in awe of the monarch—hence the concept of the perfect king.

Others have advanced different theories to explain this shift in the meaning of the maxim. One suggestion is that it came into being with the accession to the throne of Henry III as a lad of nine in 1216.[9] Responsibility for the selection of ministers fell to the national council until Henry was almost twenty, and in this case legal responsibility followed real power (at least until Henry came of age). Because the young monarch was not actually responsible for the choice of his ministers, he was not legally responsible for their actions. His "subordinates," who did the actual choosing, could be held legally responsible, but he could not.

A third approach looks to the nature of the feudal courts and their jurisdiction. Numerous writers have noted that the lord of the manor was not subject to the jurisdiction of his own courts.[10] In the case of most noblemen a higher court (the king's) was available, but the monarch (in his fortunate position atop the feudal pyramid) had no courts above his own; hence he could not be called into court. Under this explanation the maxim states the simple result of the normal application of the feudal system rules.

Blackstone uses a variant of this jurisdictional explanation to buttress his "noble lie" rationale. The law ascribes sovereignty to the king, he writes, and declares him to be "the supreme head of the realm in matters both civil and ecclesiastical, and of consequence inferior to no man upon earth, dependent on no man, accountable to no man."[11] The practical element quickly follows:

Hence it is, that no suit or action can be brought against the king, even in civil matters, because no court can have jurisdiction over him. For all jurisdiction implies superiority of power: authority to try would be vain and idle, without an authority to address; and the sentence of a court would be contemptible, unless that court had the power to command the execution of it: but who, says Finch, shall command the king?[12]

As a practical matter there was no force in England that could impose its will upon the monarch, and so far as Blackstone is concerned the theory of the law—the "modern" view of the maxim—properly followed reality.

It does seem to be a matter of fairly general agreement, however, that this view of the doctrine did not come into full flower in England until the days of the absolute monarch, and in the same period the doctrine of divine right and the acceptance of the king as the head of the church were also working to put the monarch into a privileged position.[13] This agreement does not necessarily demonstrate a "cause" for the maxim's shift in content. Rather, it more likely shows one among several that were operating to suit the realities of the times. For whatever reasons, any sentiment that medievalists might have recognized was no longer bound up with the maxim "The King can do no wrong." It had become the touchstone of royal irresponsibility.

Does all this mean that the British subject was without legal recourse when someone connected with the government[14] violated his rights? Not so, even according to Blackstone, with (for him) one minor exception. In the matter of property rights, the petition of right had become routinely available from the reign of Edward I on. Although the subject was indeed barred from compelling the king to come into his own court, the English had developed the petition as a procedural device by which he could request the sovereign to grant permission for a judicial verdict on the merits of the dispute.[15] Originally, granting the petition was purely a matter of grace, but over time it became automatic for all· practical purposes as the king routinely endorsed the petition with the words "Let right be done." Fratcher[16] has noted that a royal adviser successfully urging denial of a meritorious petition of right could, at least theoretically, have been held personally liable in the king's courts. Even with this apparent improvement in the victim's position, the petition of right was not a total remedy by any means. Perhaps the most serious limitation was that it did not lie for torts.[17]

Blackstone's second escape clause concerned "ordinary public oppression" by officers of the king. In this instance, the common law offered damages against the officers themselves. Perhaps this was a meaningful remedy in Blackstone's England, when many officers were of the nobility and possessed the wealth that would be necessary to satisfy a money judgment; but the problems of this remedy in the present-day United States have been canvassed in Chapter 2.

Blackstone recognized that there could be an unusual situation in which the oppression would become so severe as to subvert the constitution. The common law would not presume that such offenses could occur, and hence no remedy was provided, but Blackstone expressly reserved the right of the people to fashion the appropriate remedy to meet the problem should it arise.

The one exception to adequate remedies—the gap in the common law— in Blackstone's eyes came in the case of the invasion of private rights committed personally by the king. Here there was no remedy whatsoever. Admitting this shortcoming, Blackstone quickly wrote it off as a small price, on balance, to pay for the stability of government gained by not having the sovereign subject to suit because the king, as a single individual, could do little damage on his own. One doubts that Blackstone consulted the victims of such wrongs to determine whether they thought the damage to be minuscule.

In addition to the routes to recovery listed by Blackstone, certain actions against the crown were permitted as a matter of right without the consent of the monarch. The petition of right was not required for appeals, for cases challenging land seizures, or for matters concerning wills in the ecclesiastical courts.[18]

Because these remedies were available to the British subject, it has been said that "one might question whether the government of England actually possssssed sovereign immunity."[19] While this statement may suggest a more perfect remedial system than really existed, it is true that the English law did provide ways to surmount the barrier of sovereign immunity in many cases.

Before turning to the American experience, there remains one area of governmental immunity in England which has had a great impact upon the course of American legal development. Our discussion up to this point has been concentrated on the ultimate authority in the English legal system, but problems also arose at less exalted levels. In 1788 the Court of King's Bench handed down its decision in Russell v. The Men dwelling in the County of Devon, 2 D. & E. 667, which involved the plaintiff's attempt to recover for damage to his wagon resulting from his attempt to cross an out-of-repair bridge, whose maintenance was the responsibility of the county. The defendants were the inhabitants of the unincorporated county.

Two justices gave recorded opinions in the case. Lord Chief Justice Kenyon sided with the defendants, citing the lack of any precedent in support of such an action (which he felt meant that the plaintiff should look to Parliament for creation of the remedy he sought) and the fact that there were no corporate funds from which to satisfy an award of damages. At the end of his opinion, in what appears to be an afterthought, the Lord Chief Justice added,

. . . there is no law or reason for supporting the action; and there is a precedent against it in Brooke; though even without that authority I would be of the opinion that this action cannot be maintained.[20]

In the second recorded opinion, Justice Ashhurst advanced two reasons for upholding the defendants' demurrer. First: "It is a strong presumption that that which never has been done cannot be done by law at all." But the statement for which he is most remembered in this case is that "it is better that an individual should sustain an injury than that the public should suffer an inconvenience." He then describes the inconvenience—the multitude of suits that would result from the present plaintiff having to sue one or two residents to secure payment in damages (there being no corporate funds) and the latter having in turn to sue all other residents for their proportionate shares. In conclusion, he states: "Thus the case stands on principle, but I think the case cited from Brooke's *Abridgment* is a direct authority to shew that no such action could be maintained. . . ."

It should be noted that both Lord Chief Justice Kenyon and Justice Ashhurst refer to a case in Brooke's *Abridgment* (1576), and the latter considers himself bound by it. The importance of this point is that critics of sovereign immunity have made much of the fact that the decision in Russell was handed down some twelve years after the Declaration of Independence,[21] yet if the Court of King's bench found itself bound by a much earlier precedent this criticism is largely irrelevant. Of the two Justices expressing themselves in Russell, one considered himself bound by the older case (Ashhurst) and the other used it to buttress an argument that he felt to be strong enough without it. Since those American courts critical of the Russell decision's weight on grounds of the decision date seem not to have considered the earlier case from Brooke's *Abridgment*, let alone discussed it, it is the opinion of this writer that the Russell view of the English common law at the time of the American Revolution is entitled to respect as the proper view of the matter and that the starting point for consideration of the American experience is that the English common law at the time it was adopted by the first state jurisdictions did indeed prevent suits against local governmental units.

Having this British background in mind, we may shift our attention to the United States, where, after the adoption of the Constitution, the citizen was under two separate jurisdictions. Because of important differences in the position of a state in its own courts and in the federal courts, the issue of the status of sovereign immunity at each jurisdictional level will be treated separately.

## SOVEREIGN IMMUNITY AND THE FEDERAL COURTS

The starting point for an examination of the position of a state in the federal courts is Article III, Section 2, of the Constitution, which provides, in part:

The judicial Power [of the United States] shall extend . . . to Controversies between two or more States; —between a State and Citizens of another State; —and between a State . . . and foreign States, Citizens, or Subjects.

The issue raised by this language is whether it constitutes a departure from the English rule of immunity unless the sovereign consents to the suit.

Although it apparently was not a widespread fear, some opponents of ratification of the Constitution raised the objection that this was another device to subjugate the states to a dominant central government. It was argued that the state judiciaries would be annihilated, that state sovereignty would be destroyed (with states being haled into court against their will), and that the states might be forced to pay on their securities held by citizens of other states.[22]

The supporters of the Constitution appear to have been able to quiet these fears by rhetoric, if not by logic. In the Virginia debates Madison and John Marshall argued that the meaning of the clauses in question was nothing more than that the states could be plaintiffs in federal judicial proceedings. The right of a state to be free from suit was so obvious as to be unnecessary to spell out in the Constitution. George Mason and Patrick Henry[23] were not convinced, arguing that the language on its face made no such distinction.

In the effort to secure New York's ratification the same approach was taken by the proponents of the proposed Constitution. In Federalist 81 Hamilton was sufficiently concerned with the opposition argument to treat it, but he did so in a fashion that suggested the fears were so far from reality as to be ludicrous:

It has been suggested that an assignment of the public securities of one State to the citizens of another would enable them to prosecute that State in the federal courts for the amount of those securities; a suggestion which the following considerations prove to be without foundation.

It is inherent in the nature of sovereignty not to be amenable to suit of an individual *without its consent.* This is the general sense and the general practice of mankind; and the exemption, as one of the attributes of sovereignty, is now enjoyed by the government of every State in the Union. Unless, therefore, there is a surrender of this immunity in the plan of the convention, it will remain with the States and the danger intimated must be merely ideal. . . .[T]here is no color to pretend that the State governments would, by the adoption of that plan, be divested of the privilege of paying their own debts in their own way, free from every constraint but that which flows from the obligations of good faith.

. . . . . . . . . . . . . . . . . . .

To what purpose would it be to authorize suits against States for the debts they owe? How could recoveries be enforced? It is evident that it could not be done without waging war against the contracting State; and to ascribe to the federal courts, by mere implication, and in destruction of a pre-existing right of the State governments, a power which would involve such a consequence, would be altogether forced and unwarrantable.[24]

The delegates to the New York convention were not totally convinced by the advocates of the new charter on this point, however. While they voted to ratify the Constitution, they urged an amendment to clarify the immunity of states before federal tribunals—becoming the only state convention clearly to do so.[25]

By the time of the convening of the first Congress, the fears of the antifederalists concerning federal courts and the states as possible defendants apparently were forgotten. None of the amendments introduced in that session dealt with the federal judiciary's powers regarding suits brought against a state in the federal courts.[26]

Attempts by citizens to make use of the provisions of Article III, Section 2, to sue states other than their own were not long in coming. The first, Vanstophorst v. Maryland, was filed in 1791 but not reported in the Dallas reports. After hanging fire for a year and a half, the suit was dropped. Oswald v. New York, likewise unreported in Dallas, actually resulted in an award of $5,315 by the Supreme Court, using a jury. This case also began in 1791, but it was not decided until after Chisholm v. Georgia (1793). This case involved, as did the others, the problem of an unpaid state debt, and for the first time in a reported proceeding the Justices tackled the jurisdictional issue. At the time of the ratification of the Constitution, no state permitted suits against itself in its own courts,[27] but this case presented a new twist. Had the Constitution, in effect, created a higher set of courts (to use a feudal analogy) into which the state could be brought against its will? With only one Justice dissenting, the five-man United States Supreme Court ruled that it had and that the state of Georgia was a proper defendant to a suit brought by a citizen of another state. Insofar as the doctrine of sovereign immunity might be considered in the American Union, it did not reach the federal courts in this situation.

Justice Iredell, the lone dissenter, urged a judgment for the state of Georgia on jurisdictional grounds, taking the position that Article III jurisdiction was not self-executing and that Congress had failed to implement it by a legislative enactment that would reach the issues before the Court. The only language he could find in the statutes referred to writs "agreeable to the principles and usages of law," and his canvass of state and common law revealed no instance of the use of a suit to compel a state to pay a money judgment. He then looked beyond this point to the broader one of whether such jurisdiction could be given to the Court and (although he said he was not going to reach the issue because it was unnecessary to his resolution of the case) proceeded to add,

I think every word in the constitution may have its full effect without involving this consequence, and that nothing but express words, or an insurmountable implication, neither of which I consider, can be found in this case, would authorize the deduction of so high a power.[28]

Justice Blair would have preferred to have postponed the decision to allow Georgia time to argue the case, but forced to the merits by his brethren he came out squarely in opposition to immunity. Forsaking all European precedents as nonauthoritative and too far removed from the American experience to be useful as analogies, he looked only to the language of the Constitution. Urging that ratification meant consent to Article III, he found no reason to assume that federal jurisdiction was limited to state-initiated proceedings.

Justice Wilson turned to the issue of sovereign immunity in this "case of uncommon magnitude." The ultimate issue for him was, "Do the people of the United States form a Nation?" and the answer he gave was resoundingly in the affirmative. The people, not the states, are the sovereign, and they intended to grant jurisdiction to the federal judiciary in suits against state governments. For the purposes of the Union, Georgia was not to be considered a "sovereign state."

Justice Cushing, like Justice Blair, looked to the text of the Constitution, although he felt that the English experience might be helpful. It appeared to him that both the private party plaintiff and the state had an equal claim to justice under Article III:

> The rights of individuals and the justice due them are as dear and precious as those of States. Indeed the latter are founded upon the former, and the great end object of them must be to secure and support the rights of individuals, or else vain is government.[29]

If the scheme of Article III that grants federal jurisdiction should prove inconvenient, Cushing (prophetically) noted that an amending process had been provided by the Founding Fathers. In conclusion, he expressed doubts that the Constitution was meant to extend federal jurisdiction to suits against states brought by their own citizens but said that this issue was not properly before the Court.

John Jay, the first Chief Justice, rounded out the four-man majority. He concurred in Justice Wilson's view that the people were sovereign (rather than the states), argued that there was no incompatibility between sovereignty and being subject to suit, and concluded that the letter and the spirit of the Constitution contemplated suits against the states in the federal courts.

Having concluded the jurisdictional issue, the Court ordered Georgia to appear by the first day of the following term to argue the case or be subject to judgment by default. Georgia appeared, through counsel, and with the consent of the parties the case was postponed until the following term. The Court entered judgment for the plaintiff on February 14, 1793, but before damages were ascertained by a jury the state made an out-of-court settlement with the plaintiffs.[30]

With the jurisdictional door thrown wide open, and with the states having substantial war debts, the results were predictable. Suits were instituted by citizens of other states against South Carolina, Virginia, and Georgia again.[31] Also predictable was the reaction of the states, of which Georgia's was the most outspoken. In that state's lower house a bill was passed making an attempt to enforce Chisholm a capital offense. On a more rational plane, the opponents of the decision secured congressional approval of what was to become the Eleventh Amendment by overwhelming majorities in 1794.[32] Ratification was swift. The requisite number of state legislatures gave their consent less than one year after submission, but because of delays in notification the amendment was not formally proclaimed ratified until 1798 when the following language formally became part of the Constitution of the United States:

The Judicial power of the United States shall not be construed to extend to any suit in law or equity, commenced or prosecuted against one of the United States by Citizens of another State, or by Citizens of Subjects of any Foreign State.

Why did the states rush to the bandwagon of the Eleventh Amendment? The commentators on this period seem unanimous in their belief that the primary motivation was to avoid payment of the extensive war debts owed as a result of the Revolutionary War. By closing the judicial door to suits brought by noncitizens the states had acted effectively to protect their meager treasuries.[33]

So much for suits by citizens of other states, but what of those initiated against a state by its own citizens in the federal courts? Even in Chisholm Justice Cushing had expressed his doubts regarding federal jurisdiction in this situation, and of course Justice Iredell would have agreed; but it was not until 1890 that the Supreme Court ruled on the issue—long after the Eleventh Amendment was ratified. Although by its terms that Amendment does not expressly refer to such suits, the Court in Hans v. Louisiana (1890) held that the intent was to bar all suits against states initiated by individuals (without the state's consent).

Does the Eleventh Amendment, as interpreted in Hans, mean that the federal courts are totally closed to an individual with a grievance against a state? The answer must be in the negative, but only within certain fairly well-defined categories. Cohens v. Virginia (1821) stands for the position that, once the state begins an action in its own courts against a private party, the latter can appeal to the United States Supreme Court for a resolution of federal questions decided against him in the highest state court having jurisdiction over the case. This type of case is not "commenced" by the private party, but rather by the state, and thus the Eleventh Amendment does not bar federal jurisdiction and intervention to the benefit of the individual.

Other limitations on the sovereign immunity of the states in federal court include suits brought by other states (expressly envisaged by Article III, Section 2), suits brought by the United States, suits brought against state officers in their official capacities to enjoin enforcement of state laws alleged to be unconstitutional, suits brought against counties and other subdivisions, and suits to which the state has consented—consent being found in rather strange places in some of the cases.[34]

Although suits against the state itself for money damages will fail because of the Eleventh Amendment, the exclusion of local subdivisions from that ban by a line of cases beginning with Cowles v. Mercer County (1868) would appear to give some measure of hope to at least a portion of our victim-plaintiffs, had the Supreme Court not locked the door to recovery with another latch. In Monroe v. Pape, which was discussed in the context of the individual-officer liability in Chapter 2, the Court held that 42 U.S.C. Section 1983 was not intended to provide for monetary damages against governmental entities (in that case the city of Chicago). There being no other applicable statutory provision for the use of our victim-plaintiff and there having been no congressional action to modify Section 1983, recovery against entities for violations of federal constitutional rights by their agents has not been forthcoming in the federal courts.

A lower-court attempt to provide some measure of relief under Section 1983 by styling it as "equitable remedy" likewise met with Supreme Court disfavor in City of Kenosha v. Bruno (1973). In an opinion written by Justice Rehnquist, the Court again squarely ruled against the use of Section 1983 to reach government units:

We find nothing in the legislative history discussed in Monroe, or in that language actually used by Congress, to suggest that the generic word "person" in [section] 1983 was intended to have a bifurcated application to municipal corporations depending on the nature of the relief sought against them. Since, as the Court held in Monroe, Congress did not undertake to bring municipal corporations within the ambit of [section] 1983 [citation omitted] they are outside of its ambit for the purposes of equitable relief as well as for damages.[35]

Only Justice Douglas dissented in the Bruno case.

The federal forum, it thus appears, is not particularly hospitable to the victim-plaintiff in search of money damages from governmental entities to remedy federal constitutional wrongs. We once again find ourselves in the position of being frustrated in one set of courts and hoping for a more favorable reception in the courts of another jurisdiction.

## SOVEREIGN IMMUNITY AND THE COURTS OF THE STATES

Searching for compensation for his constitutional deprivation, the victim-plaintiff pursuing the path to recovery through the state courts faces a system that began with the presumption of sovereign immunity. As Justice Iredell noted in Chisholm v. Georgia (1793), and as Hamilton had noted before him in Federalist 81, at the time of adoption of the Constitution the states were not subject to suits by individuals in their own courts without first having given their consent. The king may have been dead insofar as the former colonies were concerned, but his immunity carried over to the states. As Borchard noted in his classic series of articles:

How it came to be applied in the United States of America, where the prerogative is unknown, is one of the mysteries of legal evolution. Admitting its application to the sovereign and its illogical ascription as an attribute of sovereignty generally, it is not easy to appreciate its application to the United States, where the location of sovereignty—undivided sovereignty, as orthodox theory demands—is a difficult undertaking. It is beyond doubt that the Executive in the United States is not historically the sovereign, and the legislature, which is perhaps the depository of the widest powers, is restricted by constitutional limitations.[36]

Perhaps the underlying reason for the continuation of the sovereign immunity doctrine on American soil is that the governmental beneficiaries of the common law immunity, in our case the states, found it to be a rather convenient position, particularly in view of their strained financial situation. It does not take too much imagination to see that the same forces which led to the adoption of the Eleventh Amendment could also account for the states' keeping their own courts' doors closed to suits against themselves by private parties. Abner Mikva put the matter in perspective in 1966:

In the beginning sovereign immunity was a "power concept"—nobody had to undertake a rationale for the serfs, who understood full well that the king and the lords did not have to obey the laws. It was held over in this country because it is a very convenient doctrine. No one can deny that it is a lot easier not to be sued in the first place, than it is to defend. Once the doctrine was held to apply to the government, then the sophists . . . discovered important reasons why it had to be retained.[37]

The position of the victim-plaintiff who sought monetary relief against the state in the early days of the Republic was not to be envied. His chances for recovery bordered on the impossible. American state law, however, has progressed to the point where today, at least, some victim-plaintiffs can maintain suits against the state and its various subdivisions in state courts. What follows, of course, cannot be a complete description of American state law on the subject. To accomplish so monumental a task would require detailed consideration of the intricacies of the law of each jurisdiction.[38] What will be attempted is a sketch of the various arguments advanced for the continuation of sovereign immunity, a recounting of the high points in recent developments expanding governmental liability, and an assessment of the present prospects for the victim-plaintiff.

It should be noted at the outset that most of the legal developments in this area and the corresponding commentary by a wide variety of legal scholars has been in the field of tort law generally rather than in the specific area of constitutional deprivations. For this reason, little concern has been directed toward the problems of the victim-plaintiff whose plight is our primary concern. Much as was the case with the federal courts' thinking concerning damages under 42 U.S.C. Section 1983, improvements in the plaintiff's position considered here will have been the result of coincidental parallels between tort actions and constitutional issues. Therefore, even with the spirit of reform that has been evident in some states on the question of sovereign immunity, hopes should not be raised too high for adequate compensation for constitutional violations as such.

## THE JUSTIFICATIONS

Among the major justifications for sovereign immunity are that it is "accepted doctrine," that it is a matter of necessity, and that it is a matter of logical necessity. In the period before the Civil War, it was accepted more or less without serious examination that sovereign immunity was the natural order of things. In Cohens v. Virginia (1821) Chief Justice Marshall stated that it was a "universally received opinion" that the sovereign could not be sued. Although this statement concerned the government of the United States, it could have been equally applicable to the states at that time.

The necessity doctrine is frequently said to be expressed in its most cogent form in Briggs v. Light-Boats (Mass. 1865):

But the broad reason is, that it would be inconsistent with the very idea of supreme executive power, and would endanger the performance of the public duties of the sovereign, to subject him to repeated suits as a matter of right, at the will of any citizen, and to submit to judicial tribunals the control and disposition of his public property, his instruments and means of carrying on the government in war and peace, and the money in his treasury.

To open the courts to such suits could grind the machinery of government to a halt—and possibly bankrupt it in the bargain. Once again we see the fear of raids on the public treasury being instrumental to the outcome.

The "logical" justification finds expression in the opinion of Mr. Justice Holmes in Kawananakoa v. Polyblank (1907) where he writes that the basis for the doctrine is "the logical and practical ground that there can be no legal right as against the authority that makes the law on which the right depends." Fifteen years later, in The Western Star (1922), Holmes again attempts to define the problem away. The sovereign has not consented to suit; therefore there can be no tort. "For a tort is a tort in the legal sense only because the law has made it so."

In addition to these recurring themes, Dean Prosser has cataloged a number of less frequently voiced justifications, including "public policy," the absurdity of a wrong committed by an entire people, the idea that whatever the state does is lawful, the "dubious" theory that whenever a state employee commits a legal wrong he is acting outside the scope of his employment, reluctance to divert public funds to compensate for private injuries, and embarrassment to the government.[39]

Perhaps the most flagrant disregard for the rights of the individual in favor of the sovereign immunity doctrine in a state court comes from nineteenth century Alabama jurisprudence. In State v. Hill (Ala. 1875) the state Supreme Court put the rule as follows:

> Although the individuals who have the administration of public affairs may commit very gross outrages, it is not congruous with the ideas of order and duty, that the State, the august and sovereign body whose servants they are, from which proceed all civil laws, and to which we owe unstinted respect and honor, should be held capable of doing wrongs, for which she would be made answerable as for tortious injuries, in her own courts to her own children or subjects.[40]

It is difficult to imagine a more forthright statement of the superiority of governmental power over individual rights in American law.

As will be seen in the discussion of recent state decisions that follows, these justifications are primarily of historical importance. For the state courts faced with parties urging modification or abolition of the doctrine, the question has not been settled on theoretical grounds of sovereignty or logical positivism. Almost no one can be found who is willing to provide a spirited defense of sovereign immunity from the state bench. Those who oppose changes in the rule do so almost invariably on the grounds of stare decisis and deference to the legislature. On the other hand, the advocates of change devote little time to considering the justifications once advanced for the doctrine.

### THE GOVERNMENTAL-PROPRIETARY DISTINCTION

Before turning to the recent cases on immunity, both at the state and local level, attention must be given to a distinction which has grown up to temper the doctrine of local immunity from tort liability. This is the so-called distinction between "governmental" functions and "proprietary" functions of local units of government, particularly municipal corporations. Apparently this distinction appeared for the first time in Bailey v. Mayor of New York (N.Y. 1842), and it became the accepted test of liability for torts in many jurisdictions.[41] Proprietary activities could result in tort liability, but governmental activities were blessed with immunity. The problem was that there was no common definition of what constituted a "governmental" as opposed to a "proprietary" function.

Attempts to generalize the decisions and formulate workable rules for determining whether a given activity should be classified as governmental or proprietary have been unsuccessful. At one extreme have been the "police power" cases, involving public safety, public health, and similar activities which have been labeled "governmental," while at the other extreme have been certain "businesslike" enterprises, such as electrical power systems, public entertainment activities, transit systems, and the like, which were usually, but not always, classified as "proprietary." The items falling somewhere betewen these extremes have produced only confusion in the decisions:

Manifestly, the attempted classification between "governmental" and "proprietary" functions is utterly useless as a rational guide to sensible law-making, at least in cases in which the proper results are not fairly obvious—and, of course, they are precisely the cases for which a rationally applicable test is more sorely needed.[42]

Perhaps the classic example of the ridiculous results which can arise out of the governmental-proprietary dichotomy is found in Pleasants v. Greensboro (S.C. 1926), in which the plaintiff had entered a building housing both the city hall and the opera house. Her attempt to recover damages for injuries sustained from a fall on the badly lighted stairs failed because she had entered to pay her taxes (tax collecting being governmental in nature) rather than to buy tickets for an opera house performance (which would have been tied to a proprietary, hence nonimmune, activity).

The governmental-proprietary distinction was developed to limit the immunity of municipalities, but its operation was far from satisfactory. Recovery for injuries sustained at the hands of a governmental agent frequently depended on a seemingly arbitrary categorization of the activity being performed at the time as either governmental or proprietary —and even the most gifted commentators were unable to derive a logical scheme from the decisions to define the boundaries of the two categories. It is not surprising that criticism of the distinction was widespread.[43]

SOME DEVELOPMENTS FAVORING THE PLAINTIFF

Beginning in 1957, several state judiciaries apparently tired of waiting for legislative action to clear away the accumulated growth of sovereign and local governmental immunity in tort and took it upon themselves either to limit or abolish the doctrines. The landmark case was Hargrove v. Town of Cocoa Beach (Fla. 1957), a case involving a municipal corporation. Tracing "governmental" immunity to what it felt to be its origins in "The King can do no wrong" maxim, the Florida Supreme Court rejected the entire package.[44] "[T]he time has arrived to declare this doctrine anachoristic [sic] not only in our system of justice but to our traditional concepts of democratic government." The courts had originated the doctrine, and the courts could abolish it. "Judicial consistency loses its virtue when it is degraded by the vice of injustice." Thus the "modern" trend toward expanded state liability in tort was begun.[45]

From the Hargrove beginning, a slow but steady increase in the number of jurisdictions permitting recovery against governmental units has occurred. By 1976 no less than 29 states had taken judicial action at the highest level to limit or abolish immunity at the state or local level.[46] What follows is an attempt to state the common themes advanced for the abolition of sovereign immunity rather than a case-by-case analysis of the development.

Three reasons frequently appear in the decisions of state courts which have taken the initiative in the abolition of the immunity barriers to tort recoveries against governmental units. First, there is the position that the old rule of immunity is unjust. It denies recovery to one injured by negligent or intentional acts of an employee of the state or a local entity in a situation in which, were the employee the agent of a private employer, liability would attach. To deny recovery simply because the victim happened to be struck by a motor vehicle driven by a policeman instead of an electric department employee seems difficult indeed to justify.

Second, it is frequently stated that times have changed and that the law must shift to meet the needs of the present. This admittedly activist position places the courts in the clear position of being lawmakers as they attempt to match the law with societal necessities—as they see them. A clear illustration of this decision is the Molitor decision of the Illinois Supreme Court in 1959:

We have repeatedly held that the doctrine of stare decisis is not an inflexible rule requiring this court to blindly follow precedents and adhere to prior decisions, and that when it appears that public policy and social needs require a departure from prior decisions, it is our duty as a court of last resort to overrule those decisions and establish a rule consonant with our present-day concepts of right and justice.[47]

A third common thread is that the courts can undo what the courts did in the first place. This argument frequently arises in defense of the court's position against an attack by a dissenter who urges that modification of the doctrine of sovereign immunity is a matter for legislative attention rather than judicial intervention. The Arizona court phrased the argument as follows:

Upon reconsideration we realize that the doctrine of sovereign immunity was originally judicially created. We are now convinced that a court-made rule, when unjust or outmoded, does not necessarily become with age invulnerable to judicial attack. This doctrine having been engrafted upon Arizona law by judicial enunciation may properly be changed or abrogated by the same process.[48]

Lest it appear that judicial activism in the area of sovereign immunity in tort litigation has swept the field clean of all opposition, it should be noted that the decisions often have been by narrowly divided courts and have not infrequently provoked strong dissents. In addition, not all of the fifty states have followed the lead of Florida, although hopeful plaintiffs have given them opportunity to do so. One reason for these courts' refusal to modify the doctrine in their state is no doubt a reluctance on the part of many judges to enter what they consider the legislative domain. There appear to be at least two valid reasons for the position of judicial self-restraint in the area of governmental tort liability. First, if the analysis of the origins of the local immunity doctrine in the Devon case presented above is correct (and the common law on the matter antedated 1607), it would appear that the doctrine is not solely judge-made in many states. When the state, either by its constitution or by legislative enactment, adopted the common law of England unless modified by subsequent enactment of the legislature, the doctrines of sovereign and local government immunity were made applicable by nonjudicial action. Hence, the court cannot simply assume that it can correct what it feels to be a prior judicial error.

A second reason to stay the hand of judicial activism in this area arises from the lack of judicial capability to cope with the following: determine the likely reaches of the impact of the abrogation of immunity; determine the limits of liability; provide for the method of payment; deal with the problem of statutes of limitations; consider adequately the impact upon insurance rates and the availability of insurance coverage; or, finally, solve the other problems which traditionally fall within the province of the legislature. A judge hastening to overturn the doctrine of immunity would do well to consider the dissenting opinion filed by Justice Fogleman of the Arkansas Supreme Court in Parish v. Pitts (Ark. 1968).[49] In an opinion reminiscent of those of the late Justice Harlan when he chided his brethren for rushing headlong into issues without thorough consideration of what they involve, Justice Fogelman sets out the points just mentioned and several others which remain unanswered by the majority opinion in the case. Of course the expectation is that the legislature will act to rationalize the potential chaos created by the decision, and this well may happen. California presents an object lesson with its comprehensive tort liability statute, enacted after the Muskopf decision.[50] This favorable result, however, is not always so readily forthcoming. Legislative inaction, as was the case in Arizona, can result in confusion, or legislative reinstatment of immunity can return to the status quo.[51] In the end result, it is still the legislature that has had the last word on the matter of the application of the doctrine of sovereign immunity in the state courts.

## THE VICTIM-PLAINTIFF'S POSITION TODAY

The victim-plaintiff seeking compensation from a governmental entity for violation of his constitutional rights today finds the doors of the federal courthouse firmly barred against his entry. At the state level, the "modern" view of governmental liability in tort has made substantial inroads into the formerly accepted view that the state was immune in all cases.[52] Has this "modern" view operated to secure an adequate remedy for the victim of a constitutional deprivation? In those states in which immunity is retained, the answer is obviously in the negative. The apparent trend toward abrogation of the immunity doctrine, either by judicial decision or legislative action, may extend to these states at some point in the future, but for the moment the victim-plaintiff is left with the largely unsatisfactory remedy against the officer and little more.

In the states which have expanded governmental responsibility for agents' torts, some recovery may be forthcoming. No longer is the plaintiff barred by the practical limitation of a judgment-proof defendant or by the doctrinal limitation of nonsuability of the state or local government entity, but this is only one step in the right direction. There are still serious difficulties with the arrangement. First, the recovery will be for a common law tort and not for a constitutional violation as such, as was the case with tort actions against individual officers in the state courts. As the discussion in Chapter 2 indicated, this rationale for recovery often means that the award will be minimal when the out-of-pocket losses sustained by the victim-plaintiff are small. Second, attorney's fees and investigative costs will be paid from the award, further reducing the chances for a recovery which completely compensates the victim. Third, there remains the specter of the verdict of one cent, especially for "low status" plaintiffs. Finally, the remedy does nothing to provide for the restoration of the plaintiff's good name in the way of clearing public records of information detrimental to him which was obtained by unconstitutional means or which is the result of actions based on "the fruit of the poisonous tree."

Returning to the victim-plaintiffs in the hypothetical cases which began this chapter, none of them would be able to recover damages in a federal court against the governmental units involved. In the state courts, recovery would depend on the laws of the individual state (and judicial action of the courts of that state). In states adopting the "modern" view, Dr. Doctor might have some success—although not for the constitutional wrong as such. Patricia Patrician would probably lose out even in the "modern" states on the ground that the state is not responsible for intentional torts (beyond the scope of duty), and Henry Hanks would almost certainly lose on the same grounds—particularly because Redneck had been ordered by a superior not to participate. Conrad Commoner would hardly be a "sympathetic plaintiff" in his suit—having first struck the police officer with a beer bottle. Even if state law permitted some form of recovery against a governmental unit, and even if the officer used excessive force in subduing him (which could be interpreted as the infliction of summary punishment without due process of law), a jury might well decide that he got only what was coming to him (and award him nothing in the way of damages).

Thus expanded governmental tort liability in some state courts may help our victim-plaintiff to a degree, but it should not be surprising that a nonspecific remedial provision does not focus on the constitutional violations which are the concern of this book. The judges in tort cases have been concerned largely with automobile accidents, faulty building and street maintenance, and other ordinary tort situations. While their remedial creations may be well suited to the problem with which they were confronted, they do not begin to provide an adequate constitutional remedy, for the same reasons that the ordinary tort remedy against the individual officer (even one who is not judgment proof) falls short of the goal. A deeper pocket may have been provided by the abrogation of sovereign immunity, but careful consideration leads one to conclude that it is the wrong pocket on the right pair of pants.

# Chapter 4

# The Exclusionary Rule: Is Mapp-Reading Enough?

The hypothetical cases which begin this chapter are intended to illustrate situations that might call the *exclusionary rule* into play. In these cases, consider whether the government should be able to use the evidence gathered in each hypothetical case against the victim of the constitutional-rights deprivation if the victim becomes the defendant in a criminal prosecution.

### HYPOTHETICAL CASE 8

Nestor N'Airduwell was a prime suspect in a series of burglaries in Uptight City. Although he was only twelve years old, several neighbors told police officers he was a likely suspect. Two officers, Manford Manley and Slim Smith, took Nestor to the police station for questioning about the burglaries. He denied any connection with the crimes. After four hours of questioning he still professed to be entirely innocent. Nestor asked to talk with his parents, but the request was denied. Five more hours of continuous questioning followed, during which Nestor was allowed no food (but he was allowed one drink of water). Finally, he agreed to sign a statement admitting one of the burglaries after the policemen agreed to "go easy on him." He later denied that the statement was true and claimed that he signed it only to stop the pressure of the constant questioning. Should the statement be allowed in court against Nestor as evidence that he committed the burglaries? Why or why not?

## HYPOTHETICAL CASE 9

Rodney Racer and Marsha Munster were short of funds, so they decided to improve their financial position by removing some hard cash from a local convenience grocery store. While Rodney waited in the car Marsha went inside the store to help herself to the cash. The owner of the store, Granny Goodnature, saw Marsha reaching into the cash drawer and screamed, "Stop thief!" Marsha panicked and pulled out a pistol. When Granny continued to yell for help, she shot her once in the head—killing her instantly. Marsha then scooped up the money and ran to the car. Rodney and Marsha sped away—only to be captured a few minutes later by the police. They were separated at the police station and questioned. Rodney, who was none too bright but aware that he was in serious trouble, asked for a lawyer—and was refused. The interrogating officer then told him that Marsha had said that Rodney had pulled the trigger and fired the fatal shot. He was then confronted with Marsha, and he blurted out, "You're the one who shot the old lady. I was sitting in the car like we planned, you liar." All of this was recorded on video tape. Under the law of the state involved, Rodney's statement amounted to a confession to first-degree murder under the felony-murder rule which holds that all participants in a felony resulting in a first-degree murder are equally guilty regardless of who actually killed the victim. Thinking to "get himself off the hook," Rodney had in fact confessed. It was later determined that Marsha had made no statements incriminating Rodney—the entire exchange had been manufactured by the interrogating officers to gain a statement from Rodney. Should Rodney's statement be used against him in his trial for murder? Why or why not?

## HYPOTHETICAL CASE 10

Sammy Shyster operated a discount auto repair facility in Stagnant Pond, Oklahoma, which dealt in repairs on older-model cars. Agents of the special crimes division of the highway patrol had reliable informants' information that Sammy was receiving stolen auto parts from a ring of juveniles who specialized in "stripping" parked cars. Taking the sworn statement of two informants to Judge Wesley Warrant, they obtained a search warrant and went to Sammy's place of business. When they entered the building, Sammy came to meet them, and they produced the warrant. Sammy objected to the search anyway, but the officers told him to stand aside. In their search they found seven cartons of recently stolen auto parts which could be traced to various cars in the small town. At the trial of Sammy Shyster for possessing stolen property, Sammy's lawyer raised the point that the warrant was invalid because (1) Judge Warrant had neglected to sign it and (2) the street address on the warrant was incorrect. Should the evidence obtained in the search and seizure be admitted into court against Sammy? Why or why not?

### HYPOTHETICAL CASE 11

Mickey Minor and his girlfriend Ursula Underage were driving along the main street of Tulahoka, Texas, when they were stopped for having a defective taillight on their car. Mickey got out of the car to meet the arresting officer, and he was given a ticket. The officer felt that Mickey was a trifle too nervous and asked if he could look into the car's trunk. "Sure, go ahead," replied Mickey, "there's nothing to hide." In the trunk the officer discovered a six-pack of beer (partially consumed). Should the beer be allowed as evidence in a proceeding against Mickey and Ursula for possessing alcoholic beverages (both are minors)? Why or why not?

Next on our list of presently existing remedies is the so-called exclusionary rule, which prohibits the use of the products of certain unconstitutional law enforcement procedures in criminal trials. Prior to 1961 the rule was employed only in federal criminal cases and in those states that had voluntarily adopted it for their own criminal proceedings, but the United States Supreme Court's decision in Mapp v. Ohio (1961) made the rule obligatory in all state criminal trials, at least where Fourth Amendment violations are concerned. Subsequent decisions have broadened its scope to include Fifth and Sixth Amendment violations as well.[1]

Although the rule has been enforced against the states only recently, its federal lifespan is considerably longer.[2] Beginning with dicta in Boyd v. United States (1886) that documents uncovered in an illegal search could be excluded from evidence in a federal criminal trial, the principle was first actually applied, in an indirect manner, in Weeks v. United States (1914), when the Supreme Court sustained the validity of a pretrial motion by the defendant to recover illegally obtained evidence from government custody. Of course, the return of the evidence to the defendant effectively prevented its being introduced into evidence by the prosecution—there was no longer anything the government could produce. The rule was on its way, but it would be forty-seven years before it became a rule of uniform application across the United States.

## JUSTIFICATIONS FOR THE RULE

In the period from Boyd through Mapp to the present, justifications for the exclusionary rule have been provided by members of the Supreme Court on both inward- and outward-looking grounds. The inward-looking approach concerns itself with the purity of the judiciary and receives effective presentation in the dissenting opinions of Justices Brandeis and Holmes in the case of Olmstead v. United States (1928), reflecting their unsuccessful efforts to bar wiretap evidence obtained in violation of federal statutes. Justice Brandeis urged the necessity to "preserve the judicial process from contamination" by such evidence,[3] and Justice Holmes condemned judicial participation in "such dirty business."[4] This inward-looking approach is not directly concerned with the victim and his remedies; rather, it is directed to the need for integrity in the judicial process.

The outward-looking approach to justification for the exclusionary rule shifts the focus away from the judiciary. It may be broad in scope, or it may be specific. The broad version is concerned with the impact of official misconduct on the fabric of society, and once again Justice Brandeis' Olmstead dissent provides an excellent statement of the proposition:

> In a government of laws, existence of government would be imperiled if it fails to observe the law scrupulously. Our government is the potent, the omnipresent teacher. For good or for ill, it teaches the whole people by its example. Crime is contagious. If government becomes a lawbreaker, it breeds contempt for the law; it invites every man to become a law unto himself; it invites anarchy. To declare that in the administration of the criminal law the end justifies the means—to declare that the government may commit crimes in order to secure conviction of a private criminal—would bring terrible retribution.[5]

The outward-looking approach in a narrower form is found in Justice Stewart's opinion for the Court in Elkins v. United States decided in 1960. Rather than concentrating on the results of government lawlessness on society as a whole, Justice Stewart looked to the effect of the rule on police behavior. His primary emphasis in Elkins is on the deterrence of future misconduct by law enforcement officers. The rule is "calculated to prevent, not to repair." It is not the purity of the court so much as the impact of the rule on the police that concerned Justice Stewart.

By giving Mapp only prospective application in Linkletter v. Walker (1965), the Court seems to have raised the outward-looking approach to the preeminent position and relegated the inward-looking approach to the back burner.[6] The courts would seem to be just as "contaminated" by evidence secured by an unconstitutional search and seizure which took place before Mapp as by the introduction of such evidence secured the day after the Court handed down its Mapp opinion. Because few references can be found to the inward-looking approach in recent cases, it may be assumed not to provide the primary support for the Court's continued support of the exclusionary rule. The key appears to be an outward-looking focus directed toward the deterrence of improper law enforcement behavior.

If, according to the Court and leading commentators,[7] the rule is designed not to be a remedy for the victim, why should it be included in an analysis of presently available remedial devices? There are two reasons for its consideration. First, even if not so designed, the rule operates as a remedy of sorts in some circumstances. Second, a completely effective exclusionary rule (one that would fulfill the hopes and dreams of its most optimistic advocates) would obviate the need for a remedy within its zone of operation; there would be no official illegality to be remedied. In the remainder of this chapter, an attempt will be made to (1) demonstrate that the "remedial" effects of the rule are limited to a narrow range of situations and that, even within that range, they are subject to serious shortcomings, and (2) bring together evidence indicating that the rule is far from totally effective and that it is unlikely ever to become so.

## THE RULE AS A REMEDY

The exclusionary rule can be thought of as a remedy in situations involving a wide variety of combinations of official and private conduct. It would be impossible to discuss every combination, but a simplified discussion may be undertaken to illustrate the basic nature of remedial possibilities of the rule. By dividing all official conduct into categories of constitutional and unconstitutional and by similarly dividing private conduct into criminal and innocent categories, a four-cell diagram may be constructed (Figure 2).

Consideration of the fact situations in each of the four cells of the figure demonstrates the strengths and shortcomings of the exclusionary rule in a remedial setting. Each combination of official and individual conduct will be treated separately in the pages that follow.

### CATEGORY 1: CONSTITUTIONAL / INNOCENT

We begin our consideration of the rule's remedial value with the factual situation in which the individual is innocent of any criminal behavior and the government officer has acted completely within constitutional bounds. As an example, consider the search of a private dwelling under a properly drawn and executed search warrant—a search that reveals nothing incriminating to be seized. The private individual may be inconvenienced, indeed

## FIGURE 2
### Combinations of Official and Individual Conduct

| Official Conduct | *Individual Conduct* | |
|---|---|---|
| | Innocent | Criminal |
| Constitutional | 1 | 2 |
| Unconstitutional | 4 | 3 |

even angered, but his constitutional rights have not been infringed upon because the Fourth Amendment, made applicable to the states through the operation of the due process clause of the Fourteenth Amendment in Wolf v. Colorado (1949), prohibits only those searches which are unreasonable, and the fact situation is by definition within the constitutionally approved area. In this situation no remedy is needed, and none is provided by the rule because nothing was seized. Furthermore, there would be no trial at which to invoke the rule.[8]

### CATEGORY 2: CONSTITUTIONAL / CRIMINAL

Continuing in the area of official conduct condoned by the Constitution, we come to the set of circumstances in which the behavior of the private party passes into an area proscribed by the state's criminal statutes, regardless of the severity of the offense. Modification of the earlier hypothetical fact situation brings it into this category. Suppose that instead of finding nothing incriminating in their properly conducted search of a private dwelling the authorities turned up a stack of bogus state welfare checks. Here, again, the individual cannot complain of there being a violation of his federal constitutional rights. Assuming that the court properly rejects any claims of unconstitutional action by the officers, the private party will be unable to avail himself of the benefits of the exclusionary rule when the state introduces the contraband into evidence.

It is of course possible that the private party, now the defendant in a criminal proceeding, will attempt to invoke the rule even when no constitutional violation has actually taken place, and it is also within the realm of possibility that in so doing he will be successful. Leaving aside the situation in which the judge is corrupt and wishes to get the defendant "off the hook" for improper motives, the attempt to invoke the rule may be successful because the officer's testimony does not convince the judge of the (actual) propriety of his search and seizure. LaFave notes the lack of consultation between officer and prosecuting attorney before motions to quash,[9] and a good defense attorney may well be able to cast sufficient doubt on the officer's claim to secure exclusion. It is not impossible, in addition, that a little perjury might be employed by a defendant or his associates to help convince the judge. In any event, if exclusion does occur on the facts of a constitutional / criminal incident, the rule brings about a totally negative result. Not only is no constitutional wrong "remedied," but also a violator of the state's criminal statutes is released—assuming that there is insufficient untainted evidence to secure a conviction.

### CATEGORY 3: UNCONSTITUTIONAL / CRIMINAL

We come now to the combination of unconstitutional official action and criminal individual conduct. This is the situation in which the exclusionary rule comes into its own and in which its operation has drawn the most fire. Once again, the illustration will be by a hypothetical set of facts. Police officers investigating a brutal rape secure a search warrant from the proper judicial authority to conduct a search of the home of their prime suspect. The search discloses the only "concrete" evidence in the case, a readily identifiable article of clothing belonging to the victim (who is unable to make a positive identification of her assailant). At the preliminary hearing the defense objects to the method of securing the evidence on the grounds that the warrant was void on its face (because of a careless error on the part of the judge) and moves to suppress the evidence. The motion is denied, the case goes to trial, and the defendant is convicted and sentenced. On appeal the verdict is reversed when the higher court declares that the clothing was improperly seized because of the improperly issued warrant. By this time, however, the victim has left the jurisdiction and is unwilling to return for a new trial. Without the victim's presence and without the article of clothing as evidence the state finds itself unable to proceed with any hope of success. The defendant is released from custody.

The hypothetical facts just set out are illustrative of the situation lamented by (then) Judge Cardozo of the New York Court of Appeals in People v. Defore (N.Y. 1926): "There has been no blinking the consequences. The criminal is to go free because the constable has blundered."

Had our hypothetical officers only noticed that they were acting under a void warrant, a conviction might have been obtained that would have withstood appellate review, but they did not and it did not. Dean Wigmore was less restrained in his language when he condemned the exclusionary rule as "misguided sentimentality."[10] "Our way of upholding the Constitution," chided Wigmore, "is not to strike at the man who breaks it, but let off somebody else who broke something else."

A second hypothetical fact situation will be helpful in illustrating the scope of "remedial" benefits possible under the exclusionary rule. Let us suppose that law enforcement officers happen upon a penny ante card game in a local drinking emporium, but before they can seize the cards or coins one of the participants pitches the entire table and its contents into the roaring fire in the fireplace. Furious over this act, the policemen return to their squad car and release their German shepherd police dog, which proceeds to menace the small-time gamblers; they are then told to confess or suffer the vengeance of the snarling dog. When they refuse, the dog is allowed to attack one until his arm is literally torn to shreds, whereupon he and his colleagues understandably agree to sign a hastily prepared confession—knowing that the maximum penalty will be a fine of ten dollars.[11] At trial on the gambling charge, the judge suppresses the "confessions" and directs the acquittal of all defendants.

Granting once again that Court and commentators do not lay emphasis on the remedial aspects of the exclusionary rule, a passing glance at the two hypothetical situations just presented indicates that all of the defendants were better off than they would have been without the rule. For them it had provided a partial remedy in the sense that they were not convicted of their criminal offenses. In its operation, the rule has an effect something like that of an injunction in that it prevents further harm that otherwise might occur. Of course the "remedy" is not compensatory in theory or operation. In fact, the "value" of the rule increases with the seriousness of the defendant's crime. The rapist's escape from a long prison term is surely a greater benefit than the poker players' avoidance of a ten-dollar fine. As for the amount of aggravation in the official misconduct —it matters not. In theory, at least, once the constitutional barrier is breached "by even a fraction of an inch," to borrow language from Justice Stewart, the full force of the rule is called into play. It is an all-or-nothing device.

## CATEGORY 4: UNCONSTITUTIONAL / INNOCENT

Our final category once again involves the private citizen whose conduct is blameless, but this time he falls victim to unconstitutional state action. The facts alleged in Monroe v. Pape (1961), a case involving the conduct of police officers in Illinois, may be used to illustrate. Mr. Monroe's home was invaded by the officers, he was forced to strip in front of his family, and his dwelling was ransacked in a search effort. Assuming his innocence of any crime, of what value is the exclusionary rule to Mr. Monroe? Thus far we have seen that the rule has beneficial effects for those involved in a criminal trial setting. Either at trial or in a pretrial hearing, the defendant has been able to secure the suppression of some or all of the state's evidence against him because of the unconstitutional actions of state officers. A presumption has been that the state and the individual are joined in an adversary proceeding before a court of law. What if this stylized combat never comes to pass? What if the state does not choose to do battle in the criminal trial arena? What then of the "remedial" benefits of the exclusionary rule secured by Mapp and other cases? To use Justice Harlan's apt terminology, the rule is "simply irrelevant." While one in Mr. Monroe's position has much about which to complain, we have come almost full circle to our first category insofar as the possibility of invoking the rule is concerned. There will be no trial, and even if there were there would be no products of the unconstitutional search to suppress. Mr. Monroe, and all others who may become similarly situated, simply are not in a position to profit from the exclusionary rule.

Is the rule then totally meaningless for the law-abiding citizen? Although critics of the rule are wont to say that it protects the guilty while doing nothing to protect the innocent, with only a little imagination one can conceive at least two situations in which an innocent party would be a recipient of the exclusionary rule's "benefits." The first would involve the situation in which his behavior has all the appearances of illegality but where there is a truthful, albeit somewhat less than convincing (to the police or to a jury) explanation which makes the conduct legal. For example, consider the case of a rather naive college student whose roommate leaves a quantity of tobacco-like substance in his care, telling him it is for a biology experiment. An unconstitutional search of the premises culminates in the discovery of marijuana in the container, and, although the innocent student protests his lack of knowledge of the nature of the substance, he is arrested and charged with possession of a dangerous drug. Assuming that the only crime alleged is possession and that an element of the crime is knowledge on the part of defendant, the exclusionary rule (properly invoked) in this case would operate to the benefit of the innocent defendant. Likewise, in the situation of a "frame-up" such as the planting of evidence to secure a conviction, a constitutional violation would serve to benefit the innocent party through the operation of the rule. Once again, the victim would escape unjust conviction for a crime he did not commit. In both situations the rule would be of far more value than it was for Mr. Monroe.[12]

Having surveyed the operation of the exclusionary rule in the four categories of official-individual conduct, we find that it operates to the benefit of certain parties, mostly those who are factually guilty of a crime,[13] but also conceivably those who are innocent as well. Assuming that the "factually" guilty as well as the innocent have an equal claim to the protection of the Constitution, we now turn to the question of whether the rule is sufficiently thorough in its remedial scope to be thought of as an adequate device in and of itself. The answer is obvious—it is not. Beyond the clear-cut fact that many victims of unconstitutional state action will never come within its protective coverage is the fact that even those who receive its "benefits" are far from being made whole. All of the victims in our hypothetical examples will have an arrest record to follow them to the end of their days, assuming that they are not juveniles in a state which permits the "sealing" of records. The exclusionary rule is of no service here. Some or all may have been incarcerated. The exclusionary rule is of no help. Perhaps they escaped a jail cell by the payment of a nonrefundable fee to a bail bondsman. The rule provides no payment in compensation. Invocation of the rule was most likely the result of the efforts of an attorney who will justifiably expect a fee for his services. The rule won't be of assistance here, either. Finally, of course, the rule in no way operates to provide compensation in the form of money damages for the deprivation of the victim's federal constitutional right to be free from unreasonable searches and seizures or to refrain from giving incriminating testimony against himself. As a remedial device, the exclusionary rule falls far short of being an answer to the problem of securing adequate compensation for those who have been the victims of unconstitutional state action.

The multitude of citizens who never commit violations of the state's penal laws nor find themselves in the situation of our hypothetical naive college student will not even receive the sparse benefits noted above. The only way they can hope to benefit from the rule is in an indirect sense. If, as is hoped by the rule's creators, exclusion of improperly obtained evidence operates to deter future violations of those Amendments which call it into operation, the remedial problems stressed above will be merely of theoretical interest. If there were no violations, the issue of remedies would be moot. It is to this question of deterrence that our attention now turns.[14]

## THE RULE AS A DETERRENT

Does the rule work to deter constitutional violations? Since being made mandatory on the states in 1961, has it fulfilled its announced task? If one were to employ a standard of success which requires the complete suppression of official illegality within the rule's scope, the answer obviously would be in the negative. Every time the rule is successfully invoked in a criminal proceeding its failure as a deterrent is demonstrated. Not even the rule's strongest advocates can claim that it has been a total success, yet it would be a stringent standard indeed that equates success only with absolute perfection and considers all else abject failure. The rule may achieve some measure of success without being a cure-all. The issue is to sketch the parameters of such success and inquire into the reasons for it.

In his 1970 article on measuring the success of the exclusionary rule,[15] Dallin Oaks provided a useful summary of the theoretical apects of deterrence. "Special" deterrence is the effect on one who has already experienced the sanction: "It measures the likelihood of his repeating particular behavior once he has been singled out to taste its consequences." According to Oaks, this aspect of deterrence is not called into play by the exclusionary rule as it is presently employed because the rule imposes no direct penalty on the offending officer and "diligent inquiry has failed to reveal a single law enforcement agency where individual sanctions are tied to an application of the exclusionary rule." The most that can be hoped for is that the officer's disappointment with the defendant's acquittal because of the rule may modify his future actions, but Oaks does not consider this an important special deterrent effect.

Special deterrence being largely inapplicable, we must turn to "general" deterrence, according to Oaks. General deterrence comes in two varieties —direct (short range) and indirect (long range). Direct deterrence is that species in which "compliance is induced by the threat of the sanction." This in turn suggests a conscious weighing of the costs and benefits of violating the constitutional standards which call the exclusionary rule into operation.

In the context of the exclusionary rule, direct deterrence is the extent to which the law enforcement officer observes the search and seizure rules because of his realization that the evidence will be inadmissible if he does not.[16]

Oaks is more optimistic about the potential direct deterrence provided by the rule because of the deliberate nature of the conduct involved in searches and seizures.[17]

Indirect (long range) deterrence is said to come about in three ways.[18]

There is the potential "moral or educative influence" of the law which demonstrates that certain actions have been condemned by society. There is the possibility that behavior which began as the result of conscious weighing of costs and benefits will continue as habit long after the weighing has come to and end. Finally, there is the possibility that the rule's existence may serve as an argument to be used for avoiding certain conduct when peers might wish to indulge. It may provide "something tangible to give fellow officers" as a reason. These aspects of deterrence, when considered in conjunction with the systematic attempts to evaluate the impact of the rule in the field or from court records, can be of use in attempting to assess the effects of the exclusionary rule.

While the rule has been the subject of much praise and no little criticism, it is only relatively recently that attempts have been made to test its impact in a systematic fashion. The most successful of these efforts may be divided into two types. First, there are the in-depth field studies of law enforcement activities undertaken by one or more participant-observers who immerse themselves in police work for an extended period. Two particularly interesting book-length studies of this type are LaFave's *Arrest*[19] and Skolnick's *Justice without Trial*,[20] which provide important information concerning the impact of the exclusionary rule on law enforcement practices. There are also shorter studies, of a similar nature, which concern themselves with the impact of particular Supreme Court decisions involving application of the rule.[21] While this type of study has the distinct advantage of having been penned by a scholar who "knows the ropes" of day-to-day police activity, it is without doubt to some degree subjective (as the authors freely admit). For those social scientists who prefer quantitative analysis, the participant-observer studies lack necessary precision, and this shortcoming has given rise to a second type of study, which utilizes court records and other "objective" data to produce quantitative indicators that may disclose, admittedly indirectly, the impact of the exclusionary rule in a more precise fashion. Probably the most ambitious undertaking of this second type is the work of Oaks discussed above.

Our concern with the deterrent effects of the exclusionary rule must, of necessity, be concentrated on the special and direct aspects. Those aspects labeled indirect (long range) are of course the most difficult to measure, and existing research of the types mentioned above sheds only the palest light into these dark corners. There appears to be no significant evidence in the participant-observer studies to demonstrate the phenomenon of a police officer utilizing the existence of the exclusionary rule to shore up his courage to resist the temptation of unconstitutional forbidden fruit. The quantitative studies of court records and the like of course offer no insight as to the content of locker room discussions. The indirect effect may well exist, but for the moment we have no evidence of its presence.

As for the perseverance of habit, it would seem that we could accept this factor as a given for our purposes. If the rule brings about a weighing of costs and benefits resulting in constitutional behavior, it is most likely that inertia will lead to a continuation of the conduct pattern unless important new factors are introduced which call for a reassessment of the equation, but this is to put the cart before the horse. Such indirect, long range deterrence is but a by-product of the special and direct aspects. If these aspects lead to compliance with the commands of the Constitution, the habit will be a "good" one from our perspective, but if they fail to bring about such behavior the habits will still exist—only they will be "bad" ones. In rough terms, the habit is but an image of the result of the cost-benefit analysis.

Finally, there is the moral and educative influence of the rule, which may be of importance in an indirect manner. Here we do have some evidence from the LaFave and Skolnick studies, but it tends to work against the rule's achieving the desired results. Rather than viewing the rule as a moral obligation imposed by society, the police tend to see it, along with other creations of "liberal" courts, as little short of "traitorous" to the values of the society which they perceive themselves to be upholding.[22] If these studies are accurate in their assessment of the currently prevailing law enforcement attitude, the "moral and educative" effects of the rule may be rather slim. One does not usually accept moral guidance from traitors.

This leaves us with special and direct deterrence, which for our purposes present the same issue. Are the costs of evidence being excluded from a criminal trial, with the possible result of an acquittal, sufficient in the eyes of law enforcement officers to bring about compliance with the Constitution? In the case of special deterrence, was the sight of an acquittal "costly" enough to the officer[23] to cause him to desire not to have the same experience in a future case? From the point of view of direct deterrence, is the threat of this same sanction sufficiently great to produce compliance among other officers? Essentially it is the same question, assuming that the threat is a credible one, so that no one doubts that it will be imposed.[24]

Fitting rather neatly with the cost-benefit analysis suggested in the deterrence literature, as summarized by Oaks, is the basic assumption which underlies the judicial imposition of the exclusionary rule (under an outward-looking rationale). The California Supreme Court, in imposing the rule in state criminal cases some six years before Mapp, expressed it as follows:

Police officers and prosecuting officials are primarily interested in convicting criminals. Given the exclusionary rule and a choice between securing evidence by legal rather than illegal means, officers will be impelled to obey the law since not to do so will jeopardize their objectives.[25]

Simply put, the costs of the rule will be too great for any possible benefits which might be gained from the constitutional violation.

Before passing to an assessment of the judiciary's view of law enforcement cost-benefit analysis on the terms presented by the Cahan majority, attention must be given to a second assumption, this one implicit in the Court's reasoning. This assumption is that constitutional violations will be detected—and detected in time to be of use to the victim in his criminal trial. At least two problems may be seen rather readily on this point. First, given the sophistication of modern electronics, a state officer may eavesdrop in violation of the Katz[26] warrant requirement with little fear of detection. Perhaps the information secured will lead the defendant[27] to surmise that it could have come into the hands of the prosecutor in no other way and cause him to mount a challenge under the exclusionary rule, but this need not be the case. The "long ear of the law" may intrude into the individual's constitutionally protected zone of privacy without its "presence" even being suspected.

Beyond the problem of lack of detection is the problem of difficulty of proof of the violation, particularly when only two persons know the facts—the defendant and the officer. In this situation, several commentators have found that the police are not above "fabricating" evidence to preserve their ill-gotten fruits. Burns has gone so far as to state that "Mapp, in a few categories of crimes such as narcotics possession, may have elevated police perjury to standard form dimensions."[28] Oaks cites statements from "high-ranking police officers" who admit that "some experienced officers will 'twist' the facts in order to prevent the suppression of evidence and release of persons whom they know to be guilty."[29] Likewise, Skolnick found police conducting searches and then fabricating the "facts" which had supposedly provided the probable-cause basis for the search in the first place.[30] Thus it appears that there is adequate reason to fear the Mapp rule may be undermined, at least partially, by the fabrication abilities of adept state officials on the witness stand.

Having touched on the detection problem in some circumstances, we may now turn to the central premise of the exclusionary rule: that the cost of exclusion is prohibitive to officers seeking convictions. It may be true that the cost is prohibitive, but, unfortunately for the deterrent value of the rule, there is abundant evidence that there are many instances in which state law enforcement officers act (and sometimes act unconstitutionally) with no intent whatsoever of ultimately securing a criminal conviction.

The first is the situation in which a corrupt police officer or department wishes to give certain criminal elements an effective vaccination against convictions while at the same time maintaining a public image of diligent law enforcement. The exclusionary rule gives the corrupt officer a vaccine which would make Louis Pasteur turn green with envy. A few well-chosen "errors" are committed during a raid or an arrest; and acquittal is a certainty.[31] Hopefully, this sordid set of circumstances will not be found to occur very frequently. We may at least assume, until confronted by evidence to the contrary, that such performances are atypical and turn our attention to what appear to be more widespread practices.

In his 1965 study of three states,[32] LaFave devotes four chapters to arrests systematically made without intention to seek prosecution. Some of these arrests are made in the course of performing what more properly would be considered a social welfare function, such as the arrest and overnight incarceration of intoxicated persons for their own safety. In a second set of circumstances, the police feel that they can achieve as much through procedures short of prosecution as would be secured from a full trial—and at a much lower cost. An example of this behavior is the arrest and detention of suspected prostitutes, who are required to submit to a medical examination before release the following morning. Similar "control" activities are reported concerning homosexuals. Finally, there are those arrests without intention to prosecute which are made as a punitive sanction. In the case of gambling and liquor law arrests, LaFave reports widespread feeling on the part of the police that convictions cannot be obtained or that even when a conviction does result the penalty imposed by the court will be negligible. In this respect, his research bears out Francis Allen's foreboding at the time of the Mapp decision. Allen speculated at that point:

The uncomfortable possibility even exists that the presence of the exclusionary rule in a jurisdiction may in certain situations influence the police to reject efforts to make a case for formal prosecution and to rely on such informal and illegal sanctions as they see fit to devise and apply.[33]

Citing evidence gathered in a single Detroit precinct over a six-month period, LaFave shows 592 gambling arrests with only 24 prosecutions and 420 liquor violation arrests with only 36 prosecutions, a situation allowed to develop with full consent of superior officers, who felt it to be the only way to deal with a serious problem.[34] The "penalty" involved can be substantial, including confiscation of automobiles, liquor, money found on the premises, and telephones. In addition, an informal arrangement between the police and the telephone company insures that the phone will not be reinstalled without prior clearance from the district attorney. All of this takes place in the context of public pressure to "do something" about the situation (whatever the illicit activity may be), but there is no corresponding pressure to conform to the law of arrest and the rules of search and seizure.[35]

Given the discussion above demonstrating that the exclusionary rule comes into play only in the trial setting, it is obvious that it will not benefit the victim in any case of arrest without the intention to prosecute. For that very reason, neither will the rule provide deterrent pressures of either a special or direct variety. When the only sanction is exclusion of evidence, it is no sanction at all in the cases where there is no desire to prosecute. In these situations, the police are free to violate the commands of the Constitution to their hearts' content without fear of the exclusionary rule's sanctions.

The lack of deterrence by the rule has not been exhausted by ending our discussion of instances without prosecution. Oaks' study indicates that in some crime categories even exclusion of evidence and the resulting dismissal of the case has not stopped repeated violations of Fourth Amendment standards. Using Chicago and District of Columbia data, he notes that narcotics and weapons offenses account for an overwhelming proportion of motions to suppress.[36] Once again, the "penal" aspects of such arrests are evident in terms of confiscation of contraband plus the added expense of an attorney to make the suppression motion and the possibility of a bail bondsman's fee. Unlike the LaFave data, every motion sustained in the material studied by Oaks involves a judicially determined constitutional violation. Given the repeated nature of the violation, Oaks concludes that in this area of law enforcement the exclusionary rule has no direct deterrent effect.[37]

Are we to conclude that the exclusionary rule is a massive fraud—a rule that does nothing to fulfill its major objective in deterring official misconduct? Although the information has not been gathered so systematically, the same writers who have pointed up the shortcomings of the exclusionary rule as a deterrent in the areas just discussed tend to agree that in "big cases" the rule has the desired impact.[38] Oaks' statement is representative of their views:

There are probably situations in which it deters. In crimes such as homicide, where prosecution is almost a certainty and where public interest and awareness is high, the conditions for deterrence are optimal and the exclusionary rule is likely to affect police behavior.[39]

The moral of the story seems to be that if you want the state's law enforcement officials to act with scrupulous concern for your constitutional rights you'd best be suspected of something akin to murder, kidnapping, or rape. Otherwise, the assumptions behind the exclusionary rule may be sufficiently flawed to undermine any hoped-for deterrent effect.

It might well seem that our derogation of the exclusionary rule's deterrent capacity has gone far enough to prove the point, but there are two additional points to be made before summarizing the rule's remedial and deterrent aspects. First, the rule as originally devised was thought to remove all incentives to violate the Constitution when convictions were being sought. Since the decisions in Harris v. New York (1971) and United States v. Calandra (1974), the government has had at least a limited incentive to obtain statements and evidence from criminal suspects in violations of constitutional standards. By the rule in Harris, such statements may be used to impeach the credibility of defendants who take the stand in their own defense and give testimony which contradicts their previous (illegally obtained) statements. Calandra exempted grand jury proceedings from the exclusionary rule and allowed the use of unconstitutionally gained evidence to secure an indictment. It would seem that these cases provide some incentive to ignore the Constitution. At the very least, they undermine the already shaky deterrence rationale for the rule.[40]

The second problem is one of communication. As noted in passing above, the officer whose evidence is rejected often receives little or no information concerning the reasons for the court's action. The same problem arises to a considerable degree in the transmittal of information to officers concerning the nature of the Fourth Amendment's commands regarding a reasonable search and seizure. Much of what the officer on the beat receives in the way of information comes by word of mouth from other officers (who in many instances received the information in the same way). It appears that Mapp may have had some salutary impact on police training, but the results are far from optimal, especially in the smaller forces in rural areas of the country.[41]

Consideration of the fate of the constitutional deprivation victims who appeared in the hypothetical cases at the beginning of this chapter indicates some of the promises and problems with the exclusionary rule. Nestor N'Airduwell's "confession" most likely would not be admitted into evidence because of the questioning technique employed and his age, but of course there would be no compensation for the constitutional wrong as such. Rodney Racer's statement likewise would be inadmissible under the Miranda rule. His confession without required warnings by the interrogating officers is inadmissible. These two cases illustrate the impact of the exclusionary rule concerning confessions. By reducing the evidence admissible against the defendant, they make conviction less likely—but they do not remedy the constitutional violation.

The search and seizure cases deal with "concrete" evidence rather than the defendant's statements. The stolen auto parts found in Sammy Shyster's auto repair shop would be inadmissible because of the faulty warrant, but the beer would be admissible because of the consent to the search by Mickey Minor. Shyster's constitutional rights were violated, but those of Minor were not. Thus the exclusionary rule would be applicable in Shyster's case only. He would receive some "benefit" from it, whereas Minor receives none—and deserves none.

For the reasons stressed in the preceding pages, the exclusionary rule cannot be relied upon as a deterrent in any comprehensive fashion. At best it deters in a possibly wide range of major crimes (the more crimes considered "major" in a department, the wider the potential deterrent effect). In situations in which prosecution is not contemplated or in which conviction is not seriously sought even though the victim of the deprivation is brought to trial, the deterrent effect is absent. Even in the case of well-intentioned officers, moreover, communication is frequently insufficient to convey the necessary information concerning constitutional standards either before or after a violation of the citizen's constitutional rights.

On the remedial side of the coin, the exclusionary rule does provide some benefits, particularly to those who are factually guilty of a criminal offense. Except in rare cases, it does little for the innocent victim of a constitutional deprivation. Even when it is successfully invoked, it does not compensate the victim for the harm he has suffered, nor does it operate to cleanse his official record. Because it is a trial right, it does not extend benefits to any victim who does not come before a criminal court as a defendant, thereby excluding a wide variety of constitutional abuses from even potential coverage.

In summary, the rule is not useless. In limited circumstances it provides both benefits to the victim and deterrence against future violations, but it falls far short of the remedial goal of making whole all victims of constitutional deprivations. If the present American legal system provides such remedies, they must be found elsewhere. Mapp-reading alone is insufficient.

# Chapter 5

# Federal Criminal Law: The Shadow of a Paper Tiger

The hypothetical cases which begin this chapter are similar to those you have already considered, but this time you should decide whether the officers involved should be subject to criminal penalties for their actions. Should they be forced to pay a fine, be placed in prison, or both? Note that this time you are not able to compensate the victim; rather, you are asked to consider the consequences for the individual who brought about the constitutional-rights violation.

## HYPOTHETICAL CASE 12

Victor Victim was arrested in 1972, 1973, and 1975 for selling moonshine whiskey in Tennessee. In each instance, a jury found him not guilty. Victor was arrested again in early 1976 by Arnold Agent, an undercover officer of the Tennessee Bureau of Alcohol Control. Arnold had also made all of the arrests in earlier years. This time, however, he was determined to see that Victor paid for his violations of the state laws against moonshine operations. He set fire to the house containing the still and used his pistol to strike Victor on the face several times. Assume that this conduct amounts to depriving Victim of property (the house that was burned) without due process of law and infliction of summary punishment without due process of law, both violations of his constitutional rights. Should Arnold Agent be fined or imprisoned? If so, how much should he be fined and how long should he spend in jail?

## HYPOTHETICAL CASE 13

Use the facts of Case 12, but add the following event: The result of the blows to the face was that Victor Victim was blinded and lost most of his ability to speak. Does this change your thinking in the situation? If so, what changes would you make in the fine or term of imprisonment (if any)? Why?

## HYPOTHETICAL CASE 14

Bart Bigot, the proprietor of the All-White Saloon, was elected mayor of All-White, Alabama, in 1974. As mayor, he issued an executive order which closed the municipal swimming pool to all persons who were not all white (meaning, he said, that both parents were white). Local minister Garland Gospel, pastor of the Second Baptist Church (an all-Black congregation), urged the mayor to revoke the executive order on the grounds that it violated the constitutional rights of his church members to enjoy equal protection of the laws under the Fourteenth Amendment. Bigot refused, and the swimming pool remained all white. When Garland attempted to swim in the pool in violation of the mayor's order, the mayor ordered the chief of police, Courtney Cop, to arrest him. When Garland was tried in municipal court for violating the mayor's order, Judge Roger Rights threw the case out of court on the grounds that the executive order was unconstitutional. In the meantime, however, forty-seven Black children had been prevented from swimming in the pool for three months before the court struck down the mayor's order. Should Mayor Bigot be fined or imprisoned? If so, how much or for how long? Also, what about Courtney Cop?

## HYPOTHETICAL CASE 15

Samuel Sage, the leading lawyer of Wildcat, Wyoming, was approached in his office by Sandra Streetsweeper, a city employee. She wanted to know whether she had the power to sweep the sidewalk leading to the house of Edna Eccentric, the local recluse, to remove some odor-producing "rags" which were piled near the street. Sage assured her that if the rags were producing an offensive odor they amounted to a public nuisance and should be removed. Thus advised, Sandra swept the rags into the street and had them hauled to the city dump where they were burned. It turned out later that the "rags" were tapestries and that the odor was the temporary result of an expensive cleaning process. It was also discovered that under state law the city had no power to remove—let alone destroy—the items. Sandra's actions thus amounted to the unauthorized taking of property. Should she be fined or imprisoned?

Our consideration of existing legal remedies so far has been confined largely to civil proceedings. The one venture into the criminal law area has been to consider the operation of the exclusionary rule. In this chapter our attention will shift to the section of the federal criminal law which relates most directly to state officer violations of federal constitutional rights. For the most part, criminal proceedings are not remedial in the sense of providing compensation. The victim normally receives no tangible benefit from the conviction of his malefactor, and the conviction does not erase the victim's arrest record, clear his name, or the like. For these reasons, this chapter will be largely concerned with the deterrent effect of the federal criminal law with regard to constitutional violations.

## VICTIM COMPENSATION

Before turning to the question of deterrence, however, note should be taken of the fact that the United States Code is not totally barren of provisions for the use of fines to compensate victims. Seduction of a female passenger on an American vessel during a voyage by an employee of that vessel is made a criminal offense by 18 U.S.C. Section 2198, and a maximum penalty of one year's imprisonment and a fine of $1,000 is established. By the terms of 18 U.S.C. Section 3614, the court may direct that the fine be paid to the victim:

When a person is convicted of a violation of section 2198 of this title and fined, the court may direct that the amount of the fine, when paid, be paid for the use of the female seduced, or her child, if she have any.

A somewhat similar arrangement is provided in 18 U.S.C. Section 3613, which provides that fines collected for violations of 18 U.S.C. Sections 1885 and 1886, setting timber and grass fires on property under the jurisdiction of the United States, shall be paid to the "public-school fund of the county in which the lands where the offense were committed are situated."

Admittedly these two provisions are not much in the way of a start toward adequate victim compensation, especially since there appear to be no reported cases under either statute, but they do at least indicate that federal criminal law may be used to compensate the victims of a federal crime. Congress in its wisdom having been more solicitous of the victim of seafaring seduction than of the victim of constitutional deprivation (whether by land or by sea), however, there is no direct benefit to those whose plight is the primary object of our concern. At best, these two statutes provide a feeble precedent for future congressional action to compensate the victims of constitutional deprivations through collected fines.

On the surface it might seem advisable to urge congressional (or state legislative) extension of the practice of paying fines to victims in the realm of constitutional deprivations. First, the extension would fulfill one of the principal remedial goals, at least in part: the victim would receive some compensation for the harm suffered. Second, the compensation would come at no direct cost to the victim: because prosecution of crimes is a public matter, there would be no attorney's fees, court costs, or other expenses to be paid by the victim of the deprivation.

On the debit side of the ledger, we once again find the problem of collectability. Also, there is the problem of an increased burden of proof. By moving from the civil action to a criminal proceeding the standard is shifted from preponderance of the evidence to guilt beyond a reasonable doubt. In all likelihood this change would decrease the ultimate chance of the victim's receiving compensation.

The key factor, however, is bound up with the no-cost aspect of the plan which appeared as a favorable point above. Unlike the civil action, in which the victim-plaintiff serves as the initiator of the suit, the criminal sanction requires that the state institute proceedings against one of its own officers. This is the key to the whole scheme, for if there are no prosecutions there can be no compensation of victims through the criminal law.

The incidence of prosecution is also crucial in the deterrent effect that the criminal law will have on unconstitutional behavior by state officers. If there is to be deterrence there must be at least the real possibility of prosecution. Given the lamentable failure of the criminal law to eliminate antisocial behavior in general, it would be naive to think that criminal statutes, standing alone without enforcement, will eliminate constitutional deprivations. Without a solid enforcement effort there can be neither compensation nor deterrence through the criminal law. The issue to be resolved is whether such zealous enforcement is present in the American system.

## THE STATUTE AND ITS CONSTRUCTION[1]

A product of Reconstruction, the ancestor of the present 18 U.S.C. Section 242 emerged from the Radical Republican-dominated Congress in the form of the Act of April 9, 1866, 14 Stat. 27. The current statutory language provides:

Whoever, under color of any law, statute, ordinance, regulation, or custom, willfully subjects any inhabitant of any State, Territory, or District to the deprivation of any rights, privileges, or immunities secured or protected by the Constitution or laws of the United States, or to different punishments, pains, or penalties, on account of such inhabitant being an alien, or by reason for his color, or race, than are prescribed for the punishment of citizens, shall be fined not more than $1,000 or imprisoned not more than one year, or both; and if death results shall be subject to imprisonment for any term of years or for life.

Unwilling to rely on local authorities (who all too often were personally involved in racially motivated acts of terror) to enforce state law for the protection of federal rights, Congress provided for separate federal enforcement as a device to cure the harassment and terror being employed against the newly freed Blacks in the South.

Although the original statutory language may have seemed sufficiently broad to support vigorous federal enforcement on a grand scale, actual practice did not live up to the expectations of the Act's drafters. Not until 1883 did the Supreme Court have occasion to treat the criminal provision, and even then the remarks were by way of dictum. In the course of his opinion in the Civil Rights Cases (1883), emasculating the portions of Reconstruction civil rights legislation dealing with purely private actions, Justice Bradley indicated the Court's approval of the criminal penalties provided for by Congress in the event state action were involved. Following this dictum, the statute remained for all practical purposes dormant at the Supreme Court level for the next sixty years.[2] Thus for a total of seventy-five years the predecessors of Section 242 remained on the statute books without benefit of authoritative construction by the nation's highest tribunal. Even in 1944, three members of the Court were accurate in stating that "for all practical purposes it has remained a dead letter all these years."[3]

When the Roosevelt Court finally received the first cases calling for interpretation of the forerunner of Section 242, it faced three important questions. First, what constitutes action "under color of" state law? Second, what meaning is carried by the word "willfully" in the first sentence of the section? And third, what rights are "secured or protected by" the Constitution? The answers provided by the Court would largely decide the fate of Section 242 as a viable tool for the protection of federal constitutional rights against infringement by state officials.

United States v. Classic (1941) was the vehicle for the Court's first construction of the section. The case came on direct appeal by the United

States from a federal district court order sustaining a demurrer to an indictment against Louisiana election commissioners who were alleged to have altered some ninety-seven ballots in a primary election for Congress. The trial judge ruled Section 242 inapplicable to the facts and unconstitutional if applicable. Under the terms of the direct review statute, the Court limited itself to consideration of the district court rulings on construction and validity of the statute. Writing for the four-man majority, Justice Stone dealt with two of the issues sketched above in a fashion which promised a broad federal power to protect individual rights. He concluded that the right to vote, and the corollary right to have one's vote counted, was one of those "secured or protected" by the Constitution under the provisions of Article I, Sections 2 and 4. The fact that this case involved a primary election was of no consequence to the constitutional protection afforded, as seen by Stone. Thus those whose ballots allegedly had been altered and miscounted had been deprived of a federally secured right—and one test of Section 242 had been met.[4]

Having found the deprivation of a federally secured right, the majority turned to the meaning of "under color of . . . law." Two plausible interpretations of the phrase were available, one which would confer broad enforcement power on the national government and another which would give the Act relatively narrow scope. Stone opted for the broad interpretation. Rejecting the view that "under color of . . . law" meant only those activities affirmatively sanctioned by state law, he wrote: "Misuse of power, possessed by virtue of state law and made possible only because the wrongdoer is clothed with the authority of state law, is action taken 'under color of' state law."[5] Under this construction of the section a federal prosecutor could seek indictments for deprivations of federally secured rights even when the state officer in question had acted in violation of state law. So long as the alleged deprivation was in some way related to his official capacity, the "under color of . . . law" test was met. Given the well-known reluctance of states to prosecute their own officers for civil rights violations, it is fair to say that Stone's choice may well have been between federal criminal enforcement and no enforcement at all. The Court's choice left open the very real possibility of an active federal enforcement program designed to protect individuals from constitutional violations at the hands of state officers.

The word "willfully" did not play a major part in the Classic decision for the majority—other than as a way to meet the issue of potential vagueness of the statute raised by the dissenters. Justice Douglas (writing for himself and Justices Black and Murphy) argued that the statute was overbroad. Although he confined most of his dissent to Section 241, dealing with private conspiracies, a reference to Section 242 on page 332 of the dissent apparently includes it within his reasoning. While willing to accept the power of Congress to deal with primary elections for federal office, Douglas argued that "A crime, no matter how offensive, should not be spelled out from such vague inferences."[6] Even though Douglas was unsuccessful in this first skirmish over the lack of specificity of the section, he would in three short years be able to parlay his misgivings into a position supported by five members of the Court and by so doing effectively undermine the apparently far-reaching promise of federal enforcement.[7]

Douglas' chance came in Screws v. United States (1944), a case involving a deprivation of rights which made Classic pale by comparison. The victims in that first case lost their votes in a primary election; the victim in Screws lost his very life. Screws, the sheriff of Baker County, Georgia, and two law enforcement cohorts were found guilty of depriving one Robert Hall, a young Negro, of his life and opportunity for trial before a state court without due process of law (thus violating his Fourteenth Amendment rights) by beating him for from fifteen to twenty minutes (when he was handcuffed and after he had been knocked to the ground) until he was rendered unconscious. Within the hour Hall died from the injuries he sustained at the hands of those sworn to uphold the law.[8]

On two issues the Screws majority followed in the broad swath cut by Stone in Classic. Once again the Court rejected an attempt to narrow the "under color of . . . law" language to include only those acts affirmatively sanctioned by the laws of the state. "It is clear that under 'color' of law means under 'pretense' of law."[9] And once again the Court was willing to give broad meaning to the phrase "rights secured or protected by the Constitution." Deprivations of life, liberty, or property without due process of law, in violation of the Fourteenth Amendment, were held to be within the scope of Section 242, and this brought multitudes of sins within the reach of federal criminal prosecution. It was precisely this expanse which gave Douglas pause. For one who had been troubled by the election violations in Classic by the lack of precision in the penal statute, the denial of "due process of law" was far too uncertain to accept as a standard of criminality. After all, even the members of the Court could not agree on its meaning. The "broad and fluid definition of due process" provided no acceptable guide to the action of the state officer. Yet Douglas was also unwilling to strike down the statute which might bring to justice the perpetrators of such shocking official misconduct. Rather, he sought a middle ground made possible by the failure of the trial judge to stress the word "willfully" in his jury instructions. To give the Act the requisite specificity, Douglas interpreted the word "willfully" to mean specific intent to deprive the victim of some federally secured right made definite by judicial interpretation "or other rule of law," and by so doing he attempted to escape the problem of lack of advance warning to one whose actions might contravene Section 242. "He who defies a decision interpreting the Constitution knows precisely what he is doing," wrote Justice Douglas for the plurality of the Court which joined his opinion.

Douglas' views became the majority position only with considerable difficulty. Stone (now Chief Justice) joined his opinion, as did Justices Black and Reed, but it was the vote of Justice Rutledge that converted the plurality into a five-man majority. Although his personal preference was to affirm the convictions outright, Rutledge realized that, given the distribution of the other Justices' preferences, this course would deadlock the Court. Preferring solution to deadlock, and because he found his views closer to those of Douglas than to those of the dissenters, Rutledge cast the deciding vote to reverse and remand. In this less than convincing fashion, Douglas' "specific intent" interpretation of Section 242 became the prevailing view.

Justice Murphy—the father of the Civil Rights Section (now Division) in the Department of Justice, the agency which has resurrected Section 242—was appalled by the Douglas approach. Preferring to affirm the convictions outright, he dissented. Three other Justices—Roberts, Frankfurter, and Jackson—filed a single dissent.[10] They again argued for the narrower view of "under color of" and objected to the unearthing of a statute that had "remained a dead letter all these years."[11]

In Screws, Section 242 had survived another attack—but at what a price! The section was upheld, but the rationale employed would make prosecutions exceptionally difficult because of the increased burden on the prosecution.[12] Not only must the government prove beyond a reasonable doubt that the defendant committed the acts which constituted the deprivation; it must also prove, again beyond a reasonable doubt, that the perpetrator intended to bring about that particular deprivation. The decision in Screws, while it gave the government some measure of success, did not augur well for future enforcement. As C. Herman Pritchett noted:

While the Civil Rights Section considered the Screws decision a victory, the legislation construed there can never be a very strong reed for a positive program of federal protection of civil rights, and the Court will never be free from difficulties in interpreting it.[13]

Before passing to a discussion of the enforcement success, or relative lack thereof, achieved in the last ten years under Section 242, there are two additional Supreme Court decisions interpreting the statute which are of importance, although neither restores the section to anything like its pre-Screws potency. Williams v. United States (1951) held, 5-4, that securing a confession by force and violence constitutes a violation of Section 242. According to Justice Douglas, who once again spoke for the Court:

It is as plain as a pikestaff that the present confessions would not be allowed in evidence whatever the school of thought concerning the scope and meaning of the Due Process Clause. This is the classic use of force to make a man testify against himself. The result is as plain as if the rack, the wheel, and the thumb screw—the ancient methods of securing evidence by torture—were used to compel the confession.[14]

Insofar as "willfully" was concerned under such circumstances, according to the majority, "Petitioner and his associates acted willfully and purposefully; their aim was precisely to deny the protection that the Constitution affords."

Of the four dissents, Justice Black dissented without opinion, and Justices Frankfurter, Jackson, and Minton dissented for the reasons set out in the three-man dissenting opinion in Screws.

The final Supreme Court decision concerning Section 242 that is important for our purposes is United States v. Price (1966), which arose out of the murders of civil rights workers near Philadelphia, Mississippi, in 1964. The issue of importance here was the scope of "under color of . . . law" when the indictment alleged that private parties and a deputy sheriff acted in concert to deprive their victims of federally protected rights. The Court held that Section 242 was sufficiently broad to reach private parties as well as state officers in this situation.

Private persons, jointly engaged with state officials, in the prohibited action, are acting "under color" of law for purposes of this statute. To act "under color" of law does not require that the accused be an officer of the State. It is enough that he is a willful participant in joint acitvity with the State or its agents.

. . . . . . . . . . . . . . . . . .

Those who took advantage of participation by state officers in accomplishment of the foul purpose alleged must suffer the consequences of that participation. In effect, if the allegations are true, they were participants in official lawlessness, acting in willful concert with state officers and hence under color of law.[15]

The Price case also opened the possibility of another route for federal prosecution of state officers who violate the federal rights of their victims, holding that 18 U.S.C. Section 241 is applicable to state officers as well as private parties. The importance of this holding requires a brief comment on United States v. Williams (1951), in which the Court, by a 5-4 vote, sustained the reversal of a state officer's conviction under Section 241.[16] Four Justices concluded that Section 242 was intended to occupy the field with regard to official action and that Section 241 therefore was applicable only to private actions. Justice Black, who cast the fifth vote, concurred in the result on res judicata grounds. The four dissenters argued that the two sections were meant to go hand-in-hand and that there was no decision to the contrary by any court prior to the Court of Appeals holding in the instant case.

The fact that the Williams Court split four to four on the scope of section 241's application did not escape the dissenters when a second opportunity presented itself in Price. After reciting the even division of the Court on the issue in its previous attempt to settle the point, Justice Douglas for the Court concluded that "it is incumbent upon us to read [section] 241 with full credit to its language. Nothing in the prior decisions of this Court or of other courts which have considered the matter stands in the way of that conclusion."[17] With these words the Court opened the way (or reopened it) for the use of Section 241 against officers of the state who deprive individuals of their federal constitutional rights. Of perhaps the greatest importance from the enforcement point of view is that Section 241 carried penalties ten times as severe as Section 242 (except in the case of the death of a victim). Lest it seem that a vast new avenue has been opened by Price because of the absence of "willfully" in Section 241, attention is directed to footnote 20 in the opinion of the Court, in which Douglas reaffirms the necessity for specific intent in criminal prosecutions for deprivation of federally secured rights, even under Section 241.

By way of summary, the construction of Section 242 by the Supreme Court, beginning with Classic in 1941, has presented a less than satisfactory solution for those favoring a vigorous federal enforcement program. Classic and Screws rejected the narrow view of "under color of . . . law" in favor of one which reaches even official acts of misconduct which violate state law, and Screws adopted the view that Section 242's breadth reaches that of "due process of law" under the Fourteenth Amendment. These points, scoring for a broad federal enforcement power, were countered by the Screws inclusion of a specific-intent requirement through interpretation of the world "willfully" in the statute, which makes successful prosecution more difficult. The Williams and Price cases indicate that the Court has not made successful prosecution impossible, but at the same time they allowed the majority to reassert its demand for the specific intent standard, even for prosecutions under Section 241.

## THE LEVEL OF ENFORCEMENT OF SECTION 242: 1966-1975

Having traced the doctrinal development of Section 242 at the Supreme Court level, we turn now to enforcement efforts and their results. For the purpose of this analysis, the period selected is the ten-year period 1966-1975.[18] Basic data were provided by the Administrative Office of the United States Courts concerning disposition of cases in the United States district courts, but unfortunately the records maintained do not distinguish between individual sections of Title 18 relating to civil rights violations; rather, Sections 241-244 are combined into a single "civil rights" category.[19] Nevertheless, this information can provide at least a general impression of the zeal for prosecution and the level of success achieved at the trial court level.

It is fair to assume that those defendants with whom we are concerned —state officers—make up less than the whole of the total; thus the composite figures are likely substantially in excess of the number of state officers indicted and tried during the period in question. If the figures show a substantial prosecution and conviction rate, the findings may be suspect on the grounds that it is not certain how many persons tried and convicted were private individuals not acting in any governmental capacity. On the other hand, if the figures reveal a minuscule prosecution and conviction effort, this shortcoming in the data would only tend to suggest that the true level of enforcement is most likely even less impressive.

In the ten-year period 1966-1975, the federal district courts disposed of cases involving a total of 908 defendants charged under 18 U.S.C. Sections 241-244. Of these defendants, no less than 65.2% escaped conviction altogether. Of the 592 not convicted, 313 were found not guilty by juries, 31 were acquitted after trial to the court alone, and the remaining 241 secured dismissal of the charges against them. On the conviction side of the ledger, 29 defendants were convicted after trial to the court alone, juries convicted 95, and 192 entered pleas of guilty or nolo contendere for a total of 316 convictions (34.8%). These data, by year, are presented in Table 1.

The total number of defendants disposed of for the period in question is less than impressive, to say the least, when compared with prosecutions for other federal offenses. The ten-year total of civil rights prosecutions disposed of amounts to less than 13% of the federal drug law offenders tried in the last single year (1975).[20] Even the "bumper crop" of civil rights prosecutions in 1975 (a total of 121 defendants) measures up poorly on a single-year comparison basis. In the same year, there were over 60 times as many drug law defendants disposed of (7,331), twice as many Selective Service Act violators (274), and even the migratory bird laws drew three times as many defendants (367), and these comparisons are based on total numbers of civil rights defendants (not all of whom were state officers).[21]

## TABLE 1
### Defendants Charged with Violations of 18 U.S.C. Sections 241–244 Disposed of in United States District Courts, Fiscal Years 1966–1975

| Year | Total Defendants | Not Convicted | | | | Convicted and Sentenced | | | |
|---|---|---|---|---|---|---|---|---|---|
| | | | | Acquitted By | | | | | Convicted By |
| | | | | | | | Plea of Guilty or Nolo | | |
| | | Total Not Convicted | Dismissed | Court | Jury | Total Convicted | Contendere | Court | Jury |
| Total: 10 Years | 908 | 592 | 248 | 31 | 313 | 316 | 192 | 29 | 95 |
| 1966 | 29 | 26 | 5 | –– | 21 | 3 | –– | –– | 3 |
| 1967 | 58 | 55 | 43 | 5 | 7 | 3 | 1 | –– | 2 |
| 1968 | 47 | 36 | 4 | 3 | 29 | 11 | 3 | –– | 8 |
| 1969 | 65 | 46 | 20 | 2 | 24 | 19 | 8 | –– | 11 |
| 1970 | 52 | 31 | –– | 5 | 26 | 21 | 11 | 1 | 9 |
| 1971 | 139 | 124 | 57 | 3 | 64 | 15 | 6 | –– | 9 |
| 1972 | 95 | 74 | 23 | 3 | 48 | 21 | 9 | –– | 12 |
| 1973 | 148 | 88 | 44 | 5 | 39 | 60 | 49 | –– | 11 |
| 1974 | 154 | 54 | 22 | 3 | 29 | 100 | 55 | 28 | 17 |
| 1975 | 121 | 58 | 30 | 2 | 26 | 63 | 50 | –– | 13 |

Source: Administrative Office of the United States Courts, Washington, D.C., 1976

Another way to demonstrate the paucity of prosecutions of state officers for deprivation of constitutional rights is to consider documented violations. For example, every time a court grants a motion to suppress evidence on Fourth and Fourteenth Amendment grounds in a state criminal proceeding, a constitutional violation has been authoritatively determined to have occurred. Using Dallin Oaks' data for purposes of comparison, we may conclude that the total number of prosecutions disposed of in the entire ten-year period under Sections 241–244 is less than three times the number of search and seizure violations demonstrated to the satisfaction of two branches of the circuit court in Chicago in twelve days in 1969.[22] Considering that these cases in Chicago involved only a fraction of the caseload of a single court and involved only one type of constitutional deprivation—the results of which led to the filing of criminal charges against the victim—the infinitesimal scope of federal prosecution in relation to violations of the commandments of the Constitution and Section 242 is soberingly evident.

What of the penalties imposed by the courts on the relative handful of state officers who have been convicted in the ten-year period? Table 2 presents the distribution of sentences, by year. One hundred and three defendants (32.6%) received some form of prison term, including split sentences, while 147 (46.5%) were placed on probation. Sixty-four defendants (20.3%) were sentenced only to pay a fine. These sentences seem less than severe for defendants who, by the requirements of Screws and subsequent cases, have been proved to have brought about a constitutional deprivation—and to have specifically intended to accomplish just

## TABLE 2
### Sentences Imposed for Violations of 18 U.S.C. Sections 241-244 in United States District Courts Fiscal Years 1966-1975

| Years | Total Convicted | Total Imprisoned | Split Sentence | 0-12 Months | One Year and Over | Probation | Fine Only |
|---|---|---|---|---|---|---|---|
| Total: | | | | | | | |
| 10 Years | 316 | 103 | 36 | 20 | 47 | 147 | 64 |
| 1966 | 3 | 3 | –– | –– | 3 | ––– | –– |
| 1967 | 3 | 2 | –– | –– | 2 | 1 | –– |
| 1968 | 11 | 8 | –– | –– | 8 | 3 | –– |
| 1969 | 19 | 8 | 3 | –– | 5 | 10 | 1 |
| 1970 | 21 | 11 | 4 | 4 | 3 | 7 | 3 |
| 1971 | 15 | 10 | 1 | 6 | 3 | 5 | –– |
| 1972 | 21 | 10 | 7 | 1 | 2 | 10 | 1 |
| 1973 | 60 | 12 | 5 | 3 | 4 | 48 | –– |
| 1974 | 100 | 25 | 7 | 2 | 16 | 45 | 30 |
| 1975 | 63 | 14 | 9 | 4 | 1 | 18 | 29* |

Source: Administrative Office of the United States Courts Washington, D. C. 1976
*Two dispositions in 1975 recorded as "other."

that result. One of the few reported cases involving Section 242 and sentencing results may be used to illustrate what can go wrong in the sentencing process. Miller v. United States (5th Cir. 1968) involved an almost incredible example of the perverse devices employed by two deputy sheriffs in Louisiana in their attempts to secure a confession to a burglary.[23] The deputies, Miller and Vallee, apprehended two suspects, Dyle and Gauthe, and arrested them on suspicion of burglary. Under orders from a superior to take the suspects to the station, the deputies instead drove to a secluded alley and sought confessions. In what must rank as a classic example of judicial understatement, the Court of Appeals noted that their "methods of interrogation were somewhat bizarre." Miller opened the door of the squad car, and Vallee turned his police dog loose on the suspect Dyle. Every time Vallee touched part of Dyle's body, the dog bit the suspect at that location. A superior officer arrived on the scene and brought a halt to the performance—but only temporarily.

The suspects were transported to the jail where Miller and Vallee found the opportunity to continue their "interrogation." To quote the Court of Appeals, "Vallee again turned his dog upon Dyle. Miller, for his part, lifted Gauthe by his feet, and holding him upside down, pounded his head against the lockup floor."[24] On the basis of these facts, the defendants were convicted, and the district judge imposed sentence: two years in prison—suspended. One may legitimately wonder what it would have taken to have brought on a substantial fine or an actual jail term in this Louisiana federal judicial district.

Before concluding this survey of the enforcement of Section 242, a few words are in order from other than a statistical viewpoint. Why is it that the number of federal criminal prosecutions against state officers under the section is so minute in comparison with the number of constitutional violations committed? One reason, no doubt, is that the nature of our federal system is such that the primary responsibility for criminal law enforcement rests with the states rather than the federal government. The primacy of the states in this area of law enforcement is in turn reflected in the number of personnel allocated to the task. While every county (and most municipalities) in the United States has some form of prosecuting agent (not to mention the veritable legions of enforcement personnel to investigate crimes and apprehend suspects), the national government has only a relative handful of officers committed to criminal law enforcement—and civil rights crimes are only one small portion of that effort. Even the most zealous civil rights-oriented United States Attorney would soon run up against the insuperable barrier of lack of time to prepare and try the cases if he attempted to proceed against even a fraction of the offenses within his jurisdiction. Without truly massive increases in the number of federal officers, both investigatory and prosecutorial, assigned to civil rights crimes committed by state officers, no federal effort is likely to bring a significant portion of Section 242 violators to justice.

Even if a significant reordering of priorities were to occur in this area of criminal law, however, it is by no means certain that the increased effort would, in and of itself, bear fruit of sufficient quality and quantity to justify the added expense. One particularly thorough case study[25] with broad implications recites a litany of problems facing Civil Rights Division personnel, including the hostility of state officials and some members of Congress, hostile federal grand juries which make the securing of indictments difficult if not impossible in many instances, the resistance of many local police departments to FBI investigations and the corresponding reluctance of the FBI to jeopardize working relationships with these departments by arresting local officers on civil rights complaints, the lack of regional Civil Rights Division offices with forces to carry out investigations (which forces reliance on information provided by federal officers who are local residents and subject to local pressures), the low chances for securing convictions even when indictments are forthcoming, and the meager sentences imposed after the relatively infrequent convictions are obtained.

The perceived chance of securing a conviction has, in the past at least, played a key role in the Civil Rights Division's decision whether to prosecute, together with the credibility of the victim[26] and the nature of his injuries. This in turn is said to have led to a "go slow" approach by the Division.[27] Given the ratio of convictions to cases filed in the ten-year period discussed above, it would appear that the success criterion has been downgraded somewhat in the Division's scheme of things—or that its attorneys have been seriously off course in recent estimates of what a court or jury is likely to do in a civil rights prosecution.

The use of a probable-success yardstick for instituting criminal proceedings has been criticized either directly or implicitly by those desiring a more active enforcement program, largely on the grounds that even an unsuccessful prosecution is likely to have some salutary effects: "Regardless of the outcome of his trial, a defendant is very reluctant to go through the same experience again."[28] This rationale for attacking the probable-success criterion is open to at least four rejoinders. First, while the individual has indeed been tried, he also has been acquitted. The critics offer no evidence whatsoever that the individual defendants proceed to follow the civil rights straight-and-narrow after their trials. Second, while it is true that the fact of a prosecution may have an "educative" value that extends beyond the individual defendant, it is likewise true that an acquittal (particularly in what seems to have been an open-and-shut case) may have a contrary "instructive" effect. This latter bit of education seems to escape the attention of the critics.[29] Third, there is something repugnant about a policy of subjecting persons to criminal trial when the prosecution is almost certain that acquittal will result. To argue for what amounts to trial by ordeal[30] for its supposed "educative value" is to espouse a principle that could open a Pandora's box of "instructive trials" for all manner of causes thought noble or worthy by some prosecutor. The spate of so-called political trials in the late 60's and early 70's which ended in acquittal of the defendants, and the attendant vocal criticism of such trials as tactics of repression (whether or not such criticism was justified), gives a taste of what could result from the adoption of an "educative trial by ordeal" test by which the federal prosecutor decides when to institute criminal proceedings. Finally, there still remains the problem of limited manpower and other resources. Given these limits, it does not seem unwise to adopt a policy of targeting on those cases in which chances for conviction seem to be the greatest. So long as the Civil Rights Division must pick and choose its cases anyway, it might just as well pick those in which it appears that there is a reasonable chance of victory in return for the time and effort expended.

Whatever position one takes on the issue of when to institute criminal actions against state officers for violation of federal statutes dealing with deprivation of civil rights, the factors surveyed above, taken in conjunction with the patterns developed in our analysis of the ten-year period under study, lead to one conclusion. The federal criminal law has not been, and does not appear likely suddenly to become, particularly effective in bringing to justice those officers clothed with the authority of the state who violate constitutional standards in exercising their authority.

## A NOTE ON DETERRENCE

While the paucity of successful prosecutions under 18 U.S.C. Section 242 demonstrates its inadequacy as a device for punishing offenders, it may be argued that the chief benefit of the statute lies not in punishment but in deterrence. This study has not attempted systematically to investigate this aspect of the problem, but based on the data above the deterrent effects of Section 242 would seem to be limited at best. There can be relatively little in the way of special deterrence[31] because there have been so few convictions. The general deterrent aspects in the short run are likewise less than promising. Compliance induced by the threat of sanction requires that the threat be credible. The ratio of prosecutions to violations in the ten-year period studied suggests that the threat borders on the negligible. The longer-range (indirect) effects are more difficult to assess, but once again the prospects are not heartening. Possibly there are fewer violations of constitutional rights than otherwise would occur because of the long-range impact of the statute considered here, but the magnitude of the existing problem of constitutional deprivations at the hands of state officers so overwhelms the demonstrable results from the criminal law that it is obvious that we cannot rest on the criminal sanction alone as our solution.[32]

Returning to the hypothetical cases with which this chapter began, the Supreme Court's interpretation of 18 U.S.C. Section 242 would absolve Sandra Streetsweeper from criminal liability. It is abundantly evident that she acted in good faith (going so far as to consult an attorney), and certainly she lacked the specific intent necessary for a Section 242 conviction. Arnold Agent and Bernard Bigot both fall within the provisions of

Section 242, but their chances of facing criminal prosecution are minimal, given the enforcement level in the ten-year period discussed above. Even if charges were filed, the conviction rate gives them a better-than-even chance of being acquitted. Certainly their chances of going to prison are minimal. The differences in the fact situations recounted in Cases 12 and 13 (with Victor Victim being blinded and deprived of the power of speech in Case 13) are not relevant to criminal liability under Section 242— although the severity of injury could of course influence the thinking of a jury. Courtney Cop, the police officer in Allwhite, Alabama, could also be liable (segregated public facilities having been declared unconstitutional in a number of major decisions over the years), but again the possibility of securing a conviction seems low, particularly with a jury trial.

The national government, for all the hopes of the Radical Republicans in Congress immediately following the Civil War, has proved ineffective in mobilizing the criminal justice process against state officers who deprive individuals of their federal constitutional rights. The United States Supreme Court, in a series of decisions, has contributed to the pattern by imposing a specific-intent standard to avoid the problem of unconstitutional vagueness in the statute so that even the broad interpretation of "under color of . . . law" has not sufficed to make the statute a viable tool for protecting constitutional liberties. In the period 1966-1975, analysis of the information compiled by the Administrative Office of the United States Courts indicates relatively few prosecutions under 18 U.S.C. Section 242 and even fewer successful ones. The section simply is not demonstrating a capacity for punishing state officers who violate its commands. In terms of deterrence, it seems unlikely that there is sufficient credible threat of sanction to deter official misconduct on any significant scale. From the point of view of the student of the American legal system, the sad conclusion is that 18 U.S.C. Section 242 has proved to be no more than the shadow of a paper tiger.

# Chapter 6

# Remedies and Realities:
# The Failure and the Deeper Problem

Our seriatim consideration of the remedies provided by the American legal system to the victim of a state-action constitutional deprivation has come to a close. Considered individually, they have presented little hope of fulfilling the goals set out in the introduction to this study—adequate compensation, guaranteed recoverability, removal of legal and extra-legal consequences, ready availability to all, and promptness. Sometimes, however, several items may be combined into a whole which is greater than the sum of its parts. Strength in one part may compensate for the weaknesses in another. Unfortunately, this is not the case with the existing remedies for constitutional deprivations. While there is sometimes compensation for out-of-pocket expenses, practice demonstrates that the constitutional deprivation per se goes uncompensated in almost all instances. Because many states retain their sovereign immunity, the only source of recovery is the frequently judgment-proof individual officer. The exclusionary rule operates to remove some legal consequences of the deprivation, but does nothing regarding the extra-legal consequences flowing from a permanent arrest record. None of the remedies studied make adequate provision for those of low status or income. The financially able may at least take their chances under the present system, but the "little man" may be left with little hope and less chance for real compensation. Finally, the backlogs in our courts today preclude prompt settlement of the issues, let alone prompt compensation. Although this point was not made in the seriatim examination, it is of crucial importance. So long as victims of constitutional deprivations must plod through the mire of congested dockets and interminable procedural delaying tactics, a speedy remedy remains but a mirage.

The conclusion is inescapable. If the "very essence of civil liberty" about which Chief Justice Marshall wrote is to be made a reality, a new remedial procedure must be established. Before undertaking the task of developing the outline of that remedial machinery, however, we should stop to reconsider the nature of the problem before us. Is the task a necessary one? Are the constitutional deprivations which concern us likely to disappear, or is this plague destined to continue as a menace to the rights of individuals?

Recalling for a moment the pyramid diagram suggested in the introduction, we may be able to see an important key to the issue. The use of a pyramid for depicting constitutional interpretation authority in the United States naturally calls to mind the concept of hierarchy, where the Court commands and those below hasten to carry out the decree. The lower courts and the officers of the state at the ground level should bend their backs to the task of securing invividual rights. The opinions of the Supreme Court from time to time reinforce this image when they conclude with the words, "It is so ordered." As we have already noted, however, the hierarchical control exercised by the Court over its subordinates in interpretation authority is far from complete.

## THE FAILURE AND ITS FIVE FACTORS

In attempting to provide at least a partial explanation for the failure of those subordinates to follow the Court's commands, it is suggested that insight may be gained from an excellent study concerned with the executive branch of the national government (which is also at least nominally a hierarchy and which certainly exhibits less than total control from the top). In 1961 Richard Neustadt wrote *Presidential Power,* today viewed as the classic treatment of the power of the President of the United States.[1] Neustadt asserted that there are five necessary elements for a presidential order's being self-executing. Neustadt's five factors are: (1) the President's involvement must be unambiguous; (2) the President's order must be unambiguous; (3) the President's order must be widely publicized; (4) the reicipients of the order must have the means to carry it out; and (5) the recipients must have no apparent doubts about the authority of the President to issue the order.[2] If *all* these are not present (the situation into which the vast majority of cases fall, according to Neustadt), the President is unable to command—he must persuade by bargaining.

Can Neustadt's five factors be of assistance in our analysis if we strike out "President" and insert "Supreme Court?" There appear to be sound reasons to expect such assistance. A commentary on Neustadt's work[3] stresses the point that the factors are operative in the broad context of formal organizations and not limited to the presidency alone.[4]

On the level of authoritative constitutional interpretation and delineation of the limits of legitimate state governmental activity, the Supreme Court may be viewed as an "executive" at the top of a hierarchy—at least in the broad context of a superior-subordinate relationship within the overall governmental complex. In many respects the positions of the President and the Supreme Court are strikingly similar. Neither possesses the authority to hire, fire, promote, or demote the vast majority of those who are nominally their subordinates. Both must deal with "subordinates" who possess independent bases of political support and power. Neither can exercise more than sporadic control over the activities of those lower in the respective hierarchies. This similarity of position is a hopeful sign for success in an attempt to use the five Neustadt factors in an analysis of the Court's attempts to "command" that constitutional rights be respected by state officers.

## CLEAR INVOLVEMENT OF THE COURT

The first of the five factors necessary for an order to be self-executing is that the President's involvement be unambiguous. It must be clear that the President himself, rather than an underling, is personally issuing the command. Transferring this principle to the constitutional interpretation pyramid, it is the United States Supreme Court which must be clearly involved. As with the President, this is the place beyond which there is no appeal within the given hierarchy.

This is the least demanding of the five factors. All that is required is that those who are expected to obey the command become aware that the Court has become involved. How likely is this to happen in the case of decisions involving individual rights in the context of state action?

Several sources are available from which the Court's involvement may become clear. When it decides a case, that fact is clear to anyone who reads the United States Reports or the various private publications which report the actions of the nation's highest tribunal. No matter how unclear the reasoning or how sharply divided the Court, it is abundantly clear that the Court has become directly involved.[5] The immediate problem is that, although most lawyers and many political scientists have access to, and an interest in, the contents of the United States Reports, it is reasonably safe to say that the overwhelming majority of the vast numbers of state and local governmental employees in the United States have neither access to the reports nor inclination to peruse the decisions. Even if they had access and interest, many would lack the minimal technical skills even to find whether the Court had become directly involved in an issue area which concerns their official activities.

The primary sources having failed to be of much use in notifying state officers of Supreme Court involvement, reliance must be placed on secondary sources. Radio and television sometimes may be of assistance. News stories concerning the Supreme Court's decisions are occasionally broadcast, but it is a rare instance in which the coverage devoted to any single decision lasts more than a minute at most, and even then the story is unlikely to be followed up in the next newscast. Such one-shot coverage may or may not alert the state employee that the Court has acted. Furthermore, the mass media coverage does not begin to touch every decision rendered by the Court, even on constitutional questions. One could sit through the nightly network news for weeks on end without receiving a single word about cases which eventually appear between the covers of the United States Reports.

Apart from the *New York Times*—not a likely ingredient in the daily newspaper diet of state and local officials—print journalism gives the Court short shrift, no matter how we might hope that the situation were otherwise. In many local journals, there simply will be no coverage whatsover of the doings of the Supreme Court, and even in metropolitan publications the treatment of the Court's work may be placed deep inside the least inviting section—or omitted entirely.

Communication within a professional specialty—either by trade journal or by word of mouth—may also bring word of the Supreme Court action, yet this is also a less than promising avenue for the transmittal of information because someone in the organization must make the initial effort to become aware of the Supreme Court's activity. It may be that in large governmental agencies, an office of legal counsel will have as one of its duties the monitoring of Supreme Court activity, but even this sort of activity need not result in accurate communication to the lower levels.

On the surface, then, it appears that there is little cause for optimism that large numbers of state and local government officials generally will even become aware of the involvement of the Supreme Court in issue areas that touch on their spheres of activity. A more careful attempt to treat this problem at least partially confirms the suspicion that even Supreme Court involvement is not conveyed to top-echelon officials. A 1968 graduate student survey of a sample of Missouri fire chiefs[6] revealed that, with the notable exceptions of Kansas City and St. Louis, most of the officials contacted had not even heard of the important Camara and See[7] decisions requiring a search warrant for fire inspections of private dwellings and business premises when the owner or occupant refuses permission to enter. The implications for constitutional protection are clear. Even the well-meaning fire chief could blunder into a supposedly protected zone, and if the chief is not aware of the Court's involvement it is fair to speculate that his subordinates are likewise uninformed. All of the possible sources of information concerning the Supreme Court's involvement in this issue area failed to meet even the first of Neustadt's five tests.

There is reason to believe that what was true of Missouri fire chiefs is also true of other agencies of government at the state and local level. As noted above,[8] the communication process within police departments, especially in rural areas, is almost nonexistent when it comes to official dissemination of information concerning judicial decisions on the exclusionary rule.

What can be said, then, on this first of Neustadt's five factors? At best, clear Supreme Court involvement is a sometime thing. It is probably safe to say that most state officials were soon aware of Brown v. Board of Education (1954)—at least to the extent of knowing that the Supreme Court had done something—but in less spectacular and less bitterly debated decisions there is considerable reason to doubt that even this simplest of the five factors is fulfilled.

CLARITY OF THE ORDER

The second "command factor" is that the order be phrased in unambiguous language—that there be clarity of meaning. It is no doubt clear to anyone who has read the Supreme Court's civil liberties decisions in recent years that this standard often goes unmet. Yet while some Justices do indeed seem to have the gift of obfuscation, the problem is not to be solved by sending the Court through a course in freshman English every few years. Rather, the lack of precision in so many crucial cases, or even lines of cases, is symptomatic of problems more basic and thus less easily solved. At the heart of the matter is the inescapable fact that the United States Supreme Court is a collegial institution rather than an individual command-giver.

In the earliest days of the Court, when opinions were delivered seriatim, (each Justice delivering his own), the source of a confused or confusing opinion was not difficult to ascertain; but that was not the basic problem. Even when the individual justices expressed themselves with crystal clarity, there remained the task of reconciling their views (or at least those of a majority of the Court). To find the rule of law in a case required the least common denominator.[9]

Seriatim opinions, at least as a matter of regular procedure, went the way of the dodo bird when John Marshall took up his position in the Court's center chair. By institutionalizing the work product of the Justices, the great Chief Justice appeared to have stilled the clamor of many voices and substituted the clarion call of the Court. Of course, in almost all instances the embodiment of the newfound oracle was none other John Marshall. Perhaps if succeeding Chief Justices had managed to dominate their fellows in this fashion the problem of clarity would have been a less pressing one, at least as long as the Chief could express himself so forcefully as Marshall.[10] Such, however, was not to be the course of American judicial history. Certainly in the second third of the twentieth century, the period which has seen the Court become more concerned with securing individual rights from state violation than ever before, no Chief Justice has come close to controlling the Court in the fashion of John Marshall. Justices like Felix Frankfurter, Hugo Black, and the second John M. Harlan were not men to be dominated by anyone, nor do the present members of the Court appear to be under the thumb of Chief Justice Burger.

Marshall's hegemony is gone, but the form lingers on in the sense that the "opinion of the Court" is still standard operating procedure for the Supreme Court. This reality has a significant impact on what is likely to be found in that document. Unlike Marshall, who apparently could perform essentially as a free agent, the author of today's institutional opinion must secure the approval of at least four colleagues, who are unlikely to stand in awe of him. This is far from automatic in the present Court. As Murphy and Tanenhaus phrase it:

At best, it is difficult for a group of strong-willed men to agree to a complex document that must be broad enough—and sometimes vague enough—to encompass all their views and still tight enough to survive the counterarguments of potential or actual dissenters.[11]

There's the rub. The reconciliation of views to form the necessary five-man majority, which once took place in the open through seriatim opinions (and subsequent analysis thereof), has been removed from public view and placed behind the velvet curtain. The reconciliation still takes place, as it must, but the how and why are not immediately evident. Only when a Justice's papers become available, if then, does the scholar following the Court begin to get a clear picture of the bargaining that has taken place and the modification of the opinion of the Court which has occurred. Given the fact that this may be years or even decades after the decision in a given case, those opinions which are "sometimes vague enough" to paper over the gaps in a less than solid majority may present what appears to be inexplicable confusion. The political scientist can take the position that all will become clear in time (as the papers of the Justices become available for scholarly analysis), but this is of little value in our present context—the search for an unambiguous command. The response of one critic of recent decisions concerning search and seizure and the exclusionary rule expresses the frustration of the "recipient" of the Court's orders: "Enough is enough. These processes would not deter or enlighten a policeman in Gary with a Ph.D. who was going to law school at night."[12]

Lest it appear that this is an attempt to paint the job of the Justices as a simple one compounded only by strong-willed men who insist on having their own way on every detail, let us emphasize that the problems before the Court are complex and sometimes present problems that seem almost to defy solution. Although the members of the Court may seem fully confident of their positions in the opinions they write, recent research has shed valuable light on the doubts and fluctuation of Justices' positions between oral argument and decision day.[13] Perhaps the most recent public expression of reversal of position is Justice Harlan's candid admission that he changed his mind in the 1971 Bivens case.

My initial view of this case was that the Court of Appeals was correct in dismissing the complaint, but for reasons stated in the opinion I am now persuaded to the contrary. Accordingly, I join in the judgment of reversal.[14]

It may be, then, that in at least some instances opinions fail to strike out full speed ahead in a given direction because their authors still harbor some doubts on crucial issues.[15]

Thus far we have been concerned only with the opinion of the Court. In Marshall's day, our task would have been all but complete at this point, but the lack of unanimity on the recent Court has been accompanied by a propensity for the expression of views either in dissent or by way of concurring opinions. Even when the majority can get together on a single opinion, there is likely to be sniping—if not a frontal attack—from the losing faction. Justices Brennan and Marshall, the remaining holdovers from the Warren Court's solid majority, increasingly find themselves in the minority, and they have given no indication of a willingness to take their defeats in silence.

Add to the continuing division of votes and the proliferation of opinions the fact that the Court is still in a state of flux from the new Justices appointed by Richard Nixon and Gerald Ford, and we have the makings of continued uncertainty. It may well be some time before the Burger Court begins to find a stable majority—let alone a common view that can be expressed for the Court.

A final factor works against clarity in the Court's commands. This is the frequently observed practice of the Court to decide cases on the narrowest possible grounds and not to go beyond the facts of a particular case. While this approach may tend to give precision to the individual case, it does little to instruct the "recipient" of the command on what to do in similar or analogous situations. In a rather ironic sense, the more precise the Court becomes on the narrow facts of a case, the less guidance it gives to lower-level officials, who are unlikely to run across a fact situation "on all fours" with the case in question.

What, then, are we to conclude? It appears that the second of the five Neustadt factors—that of clarity of the command—is destined to remain unfulfilled, at least in any across-the-board view of constitutional rights of individuals against state action. The collegial nature of the Court, the felt necessity to coalesce views into an opinion of the Court, the lack of a nearly totally dominant Chief Justice who writes particularly lucid opinions, the well-developed custom of freedom to dissent and concur (with opinions), more or less narrow holdings on the facts of specific cases, and the continuing complexity of issues faced by the Court—all work in concert to frustrate the hopes of those who would seek consistently unambiguous commands from the nation's highest tribunal.

## WIDELY PUBLICIZED ORDER

The third factor listed by Neustadt is that the President's order be widely publicized. The reason that this is felt to be important is that it lets the subordinate know that others are aware that he has been ordered to act. For our purposes, the low visibility of Supreme Court involvement undermines this factor as well. In at least a large number of cases the "ordinary" individual will be unaware that the Supreme Court has ruled on the point, let alone know what the ruling was. Even if the officer himself knows the nature of the decision, this factor of Neustadt's will be missing unless there is wide distribution of the information about the order.

In some instances this wide distribution will occur, of course. Miranda[16] rights have been popularized by several years of dramatization by such television favorites as the stars of *Dragnet* and other police shows, for example. When the commands of the Court are widely known, at least this third factor will be met. The problem is that media distribution of information concerning the activities of the Court, as noted above, is not particularly well suited to the task—or at least has not made use of its potential.

## CAPABILITY TO COMPLY

For an order to be self-executing in the Neustadt framework, the recipient must have the capability to carry it out. Perhaps a better way of stating the problem in our context is to say that the recipient must perceive that he has the capability required.

In some instances this is a standard easily met. To use Miranda once again as an example, police departments across the country were able to provide cards containing the required "warnings" for their officers. All that the officer had to do to comply at least with the letter of Miranda was to remove the card from his pocket and read its contents to the suspect or prisoner. As subsequent dismissals and reversals of convictions indicate, the proper practice was not followed in all instances, but it is difficult to argue that the failure was based on the lack of capability to comply with the Court's command.[17]

Other situations may not be so readily brought into line with the judicial decision. Consider the example of a Court-approved order for massive school busing to achieve an integrated school attendance pattern. In the case of a financially distressed school district whose citizens consistently refuse to approve additional funds it is at least conceivable that the school board simply would be unable to purchase or hire the vehicles necessary to carry out the plan. The result would be continued violations of the judicially declared right of the children to attend integrated schools. In the case of true financial inability to provide the necessary transportation, the courts' orders would do little to remedy the deprivation. Even attempting to cite responsible officials for contempt of court would be to no avail. The most likely result of the issuance of such citations would be a school board with more vacancies than members.

Between the two extremes noted here lie situations too numerous to discuss, but it will suffice to say that in at least some of them it will appear to the officials involved that it is impossible to comply with the decision of the Supreme Court. In these instances compliance will not be forthcoming from the mere issuance of the command.

## LEGITIMACY OF THE COMMAND-GIVER

Neustadt's fifth and final command factor is that of legitimacy. Those who receive the command must have no apparent doubts as to the authority of the command-giver to issue the order in question. Once again there is serious cause to doubt that the Supreme Court achieves a position consonant with that necessary for the issuance of a self-executing order. Particularly in the eyes of law enforcement personnel, the Court has been found to suffer from what might be called a "legitimacy gap."

Both Wilson and Skolnick in their pioneering studies[18] discovered a strong feeling of occupational solidarity among law enforcement officers. This solidarity, combined with a feeling of being cut off from the rest of the community, results in a feeling of distrust of, or even hostility toward, those perceived as "outsiders." Prominent among the outsiders against whom displeasure is frequently voiced are the courts in general and the Supreme Court in particular. Appellate courts are seen as "traitors" to the cause of freeing the community from criminal behavior, as "road-blocks" to effective law enforcement, and as participants in a two-front war against the police (the other front being manned by the criminals themselves). Part of this animosity may be traceable to the courts' being outside the professional circle of law enforcement. By being "outsiders," judges might well be expected not to receive the highest praise reserved for the members of the inner circle, but this alone would hardly seem sufficient to bring on the hostility evident in the characterizations of the judiciary just noted. The reasons are more deeply rooted.

Beyond the mere fact of the insider-outsider dichotomy is a serious clash between the values found to be held by the police and those embodied in many recent judicial pronouncements involving constitutional rights. Wasby's excellent study of the impact of Supreme Court decisions[19] noted that while the courts have been stressing those values which lie at the heart of what Herbert Packer has labeled the due process model,[20] the enforcers have hewed to the competing premises underlying what he characterized as the crime control model: "Lack of congruence between the two models, or between the views of (appellate) judges and law enforcement personnel, helps explain the lack of impact of court decisions in this area."[21] In other words, the police do not accept even the basic premises of recent judicial decisions, and this lack of acceptance has made the decisions anything but self-enforcing. Overlapping this cleavage is the view taken of a criminal suspect by the policeman and the appellate courts and the resulting standards of justice. While both court and officer agree that equals should be treated equally, their ratings of persons differ markedly. To the court all who come before the bar of justice are equal, but to the policeman on the beat they are not equal—there are decent people to be distinguished from "bums" and other undesirables.[22] The result is that "the judge and the patrolman see things differently and consequently view each other with chronic suspicion and sometimes active dislike."[23]

If law enforcement officers and appellate courts are indeed taking their cues from mutually inconsistent value systems, and if the value systems are as deeply held by both as recent judicial decisions and the police studies indicate, it is little wonder that the police view the courts as "traitors" to their cause. From the policeman's view, the court is challenging his most cherished values, and this judicial behavior results in a lowered view of the courts. In essence, the legitimacy of the courts in general and the Supreme Court in particular is called into question.

Add to the basic value conflict the frustration of the police officer who sees his laborious attempts to secure convictions and what he considers to be meaningful sentences being thwarted by "lenient" judges, and the picture becomes even more gloomy for the reconciliation of court and constable. A sense of frustration and dissatisfaction is not likely to enhance the already low opinion of appellate courts held by those who feel that law enforcement should be left in the hands of the "professionals."

Is this conflict inevitable? Of course, there is no way to answer the question for all time. State officials may come to share the view, currently dominant in the judiciary, that the due process model's values are the ones to be preferred, or the courts may turn to an acceptance of what now are the policeman's chosen values; but neither change seems imminent. By returning to the "outsider" concept for a moment, we may employ Skolnick's pessimistic assessment of the chances for future harmony as a fitting capsule summary:

Antagonism between the police and the judiciary is perhaps an inevitable outcome, therefore, of differing interests residing in the police as a specialized agency and the judiciary as a representative of wider community interests.[24]

At least in the very important area of police activity, then, we may state with some assurance that the Supreme Court (along with other appellate courts) commands far less than total respect as a legitimate giver of commands. To the degree that this is so, and to the extent that this lack of legitimacy is reflected in other agencies of state and local government, the orders of the Supreme Court concerning the constitutional rights of individuals will fall short of meeting Neustadt's fifth test for a self-enforcing command.

Our analysis of Supreme Court decisions in Neustadt's framework should make us skeptical of a day when the Court's orders will be self-executing and legal remedies for constitutional violations through state action unnecessary. Further, our analysis of the government's efforts to police itself (as exemplified in the criminal law) makes the hope of an adequate job through internal controls a dubious one. In answer to the question posed at the beginning of this chapter concerning the necessity of developing a proposal for a new system of remedies, we must respond that the task is necessary. A mechanism must be provided through which the individual can on his own initiative secure compensation for constitutional deprivations suffered at the hands of state officers, because there is little hope that such violations will cease to occur.

# Chapter 7

# Toward a More Adequate Remedy: A Modest Proposal

The preceding chapters have demonstrated the lack of effective legal remedies for those who are unfortunate enough to fall victim to constitutional deprivations at the hands of officers of the states, and the problem now before us is to develop at least the broad outline of a plan to rectify these failures. In the pages that follow, a proposal for legislative reform will be put forward which builds upon the foundations already present in American state law. It is readily admitted that the plan is not a perfect solution for the problem, but perhaps those who consider it will be prompted to engage in a constructive dialogue which will serve to refine the raw materials offered here and, at the same time, begin to generate the political support necessary to secure legislative adoption. Only with this final step—making a refined plan a part of the law of a state—will the remedies discussed in the pages to come be of value to the many victim-plaintiffs, present and potential, who are today largely left without adequate legal recourse.

## THE LEGISLATIVE PREFERENCE

The reform proposal suggested here is a legislative one. It is the position of this writer that the courts are inadequately equipped, both in terms of resources and of authority, to bring about comprehensive reforms necessary to develop an adequate remedy. Even the strongest advocates of judicial activism in the area of public tort liability are quick to admit that the legislature has the ultimate authority over matters concerning sovereign immunity and damage awards from the public treasury. Indeed, those favoring decisions to expand liability have often referred favorably to such judicial actions as "prods" to the legislature to do its own work,[1] yet one may well anticipate the howls of judicial displeasure which would arise should the legislature begin to "prod" the judiciary toward doing its own work in the fashion desired by a majority of the state Assembly. Particularly if the "prods" were directed toward individual cases the legislators would be fortunate to escape citation for contempt and, in any event, they could expect a severe judicial tongue lashing for daring to cross the barrier of separation of powers—and rightly so.[2]

The principle of separation of powers does not operate only to protect the judiciary from improper interference emanating from the legislative halls. Its purpose is to separate the three basic functions of government—legislative, executive, and judicial—and place them in the institutional hands of three separate "branches" of government to create an arrangement of mutual noninterference.[3] Having once admitted that the abrogation of sovereign immunity is the legislature's "own work," the advocates of judicial prodding would seem to be in the same position as the legislators who would "advise" the courts in specific cases. Neither is empowered to act directly, and it is likewise improper to achieve by indirection that which is barred by the separation-of-powers principle.

Beyond the separation-of-powers argument lies the lack of judicial capability to fashion a comprehensive remedy. While the tort liability cases would serve as analogies for constitutional liability of entities, they can go little further. The courts cannot provide for the purchase of insurance or the floating of bonds. The courts cannot directly provide for a minimal amount of automatic recovery for a constitutional deprivation.[4] Perhaps most importantly, the courts are ill equipped to fashion a comprehensive remedial plan so long as they operate in their customary case-by-case adjudicative method. The problem facing us is one that requires an integrated plan for solution, and the legislature is capable of such action while the judiciary is not.

## GENERAL NATURE OF THE PROPOSAL

The plan that follows will be developed in a section-by-section fashion. In order to provide the reader with a general impression of the proposal which will enable him to see how the pieces will fit together, the highlights will be sketched here. In the introductory chapter certain goals for a remedial system in the consitutional context were noted—compensation for the constitutional violation per se as well as for out-of-pocket expenses, guaranteed recoverability, removal of unfavorable legal and extra-legal consequences of the violation insofar as possible, ready availability to the victim, and a speedy determination of the issues. The plan is fashioned to meet those goals.

The central element in the remedy is combined officer and entity liability for constitutional violations. The liability of the individual officer will depend upon the degree of care exercised in the performance of his duties. To avoid the judgment-proof-defendant phenomenon, the entity will serve as a guarantor of payment of the judgment.

Ready access to the remedy will be provided by sections providing for venue and attorney fees which should encourage meritorious suits with a minimum of inconvenience to the plaintiff-victim.

Assurance of compensation for the constitutional deprivation per se will be built into the plan through provision for mandatory minimum damages in the case of a proven violation of the plaintiff's rights.

Specific authority will be provided for removal of certain unfavorable consequences of constitutional violations by authorizing the expunging of official records.

Speedy determination of the issues will be encouraged by docket preference and by incentives to the defendants to avoid unnecessary delay in the preparation for and trial of the suits instituted under the Act.

These are the high points of the plan, but it will remain for the more detailed presentation of the specific sections of the proposed statute to demonstrate their exact nature and the way in which they work in harmony to provide a more adequate remedy for constitutional violations. In the detailed presentation that follows, a portion of the proposed Act will be set forth, followed by an explanation and justification. A complete text of the proposed legislation appears in the Appendix.


## PROPOSED STATUTORY LANGUAGE

### MATTERS OF DEFINITION (SECTION 1)

Certain terminology in the proposed Act will be defined at the outset.

1.01—As used in this Act, "entity" shall mean the State or any of its subdivisions including, but not limited to, counties, municipal corporations, districts, commissions, and boards.

1.02—As used in this Act, "officer" shall mean any person exercising the authority of any entity, whether or not employed by that entity.

1.03—As used in this Act, "constitutional right" shall mean any right, privilege, or immunity secured against state action by the Constitution of the United States of America.

1.04—As used in this Act, "under color of law" shall mean under pretense of authority of an entity, whether or not authorized by law.

The definitions included in Section 1 are designed to simplify the language of the remaining sections by substituting words of a general nature, such as "entity," for a list of specific terms, such as "state, county, and board" in those remaining sections. Further, the definitions make clear that the intent of the legislature is to include all subdivisions of the state (and of course the state itself) and all individuals who exercise the authority of those entities within the scope of the Act. Also, Section 1.04 explicitly adopts the "under pretense of authority" approach developed by the United States Supreme Court in its Civil Rights Act decisions.[5]

### LIABILITY OF WHOM (OR WHAT)? (SECTION 2)

The initial matter to be settled in our statutory scheme is the source of recovery or, put another way, the party or parties to be held liable for constitutional deprivations. The proposed statute opts for joint liability of governmental entities and their officers.

2.01—Officers acting under color of law shall be subject to suit and liable for damages as provided in this Act for deprivations of constitutional rights.

2.02—Actions of officers resulting in deprivations of constitutional rights shall be divided into three classes: intentional, negligent, and due care.

2.03—An "intentional deprivation" is defined as an action taken with the specific intent to deprive an individual of his constitutional rights and resulting in said deprivation. An intentional deprivation shall result in officer liability of not less than one thousand dollars and not more than ten thousand dollars for each deprivation, provided however that nothing in this section shall preclude the assessment of punitive damages under the provisions of Sections 5.04 –5.05 of this Act.

2.04—A "negligent deprivation" is defined as an action taken without adherence to the standard of care which would have been exercised by a reasonable officer of like training and experience in the same or similar circumstances which results in a constitutional deprivation. A negligent deprivation shall result in officer liability of not less than one hundred dollars and not more than two hundred fifty dollars for each deprivation.

2.05—A "due care deprivation" is defined as a deprivation which is neither intentional nor negligent as defined in sections 2.03–2.04 of this Act. A due care deprivation shall not result in officer liability under this Act.

2.06—Good faith and reasonable reliance on a statute, ordinance, or other legislative or quasi-legislative enactment shall be considered as action undertaken with due care.

2.07—No legislative or quasi-legislative officer of any entity shall be held personally liable under the provisions of this Act for any action taken in the authorized course of his official legislative or quasi-legislative duties.

2.08—No judicial or quasi-judicial officer of any entity shall be held personally liable under the provisions of this Act for any action taken in the authorized course of the performance of his official judicial or quasi-judicial duties.

As was noted in Chapter 2, provision for heavy liability for individual officers usually presents an illusory remedy because of their limited financial resources; yet this does not mean that the officer should be totally immune from responsibility for his actions which amount to constitutional deprivations. A statute tailored to the anticipated resources of the ordinary individual officer, however, might well be operable.

The sections presented above are designed to provide a measure of damages which is reasonable in relation to the officer-defendant with limited resources. In addition, it conforms to the ordinary expectation of the law (especially tort law) that the individual is responsible for his actions. It provides an element of deterrence[6] missing in existing tort and civil rights remedies as well as in the operation of the exclusionary rule. If the entire plan is successful in promoting suits for damages to compensate for constitutional deprivations, and if the individual officer is personally liable even for a limited amount, the element of a sanction directly imposed on the offender would be present—and the threat would be credible.

Unless we are willing to impose strict liability on the individual officer for any and all forms of constitutional deprivation, the statute must distinguish between the kinds of official action. By considering the activities of officers resulting in constitutional deprivations from the perspective of the amount of care employed by the officer, a scheme of officer liability has been developed which is both equitable to the official and consistent with the notion of individual responsibility and with the tenets of deterrence theory.

Figure 3 attempts to depict graphically three types of official activity in relation to constitutional deprivations as defined in the Act. The first

**FIGURE 3 Variations of Official's Degree of Care**

| Intentional | Negligent | Due Care |
|---|---|---|

class of activity is that of an intentional deprivation—one in which the officer knows full well that he is violating the constitutional rights of his victim and proceeds to do so in flagrant disregard of the law. This class of behavior is the most reprehensible, and it is the one which the United States Supreme Court has found punishable by criminal sanction under the Civil Rights Act of the Reconstruction period. Consequently it is the class of official action subjected to the most extensive measure of damages under the Act. While the plan is primarily compensatory in nature, the imposition of punitive or exemplary damages in these circumstances is justifiable as a deterrent to others who would pursue the same course. Thus, the plan allows damages up to $10,000 against the individual officer for each constitutional deprivation.

Admittedly, an award of this size against the ordinary state governmental officer would be ruinous, but this result should not stop the imposition of the liability. The official does not stumble into the problem. He intentionally deprived the victim of his constitutional rights (with the same "specific intent" required by the Screws rule) and presumably was aware of the provisions of liability statutes enacted by the state. In this situation there is no need for sympathy for the officer. He simply reaps that which he has sown.

The middle-range situation is that in which the officer's conduct is of the type which he should have known amounted to a constitutional deprivation, but for some reason he did not. This amounts to the ordinary situation of negligent behavior in tort law—a situation which ordinarily visits the actor with civil liability in damages for the consequences of his actions. The state officer deserves no total exemption from liability in this instance, yet it is not our aim to subject him to financial ruin. Rather, the proposal limits his liability to a maximum of $250 for each constitutional deprivation. This amount, while not financially disastrous, certainly would be sufficient to inform the official that a sanction had been imposed upon him for his negligent conduct and provide him with an incentive to maintain a higher standard of care in the future; at the same time, it would alert his colleagues that they, too, are subject to liability for similar actions.[7]

Because not all negligent behavior is equally blameworthy, the statute does not impose the $250 maximum liability automatically. Rather, it leaves the amount in excess of $100 to the discretion of the court. A minimal amount ($100) is provided to make certain that the negligent officer is not allowed to escape without some contribution to the amount awarded in damages.

The standard of care required by the statute takes into consideration the training the officer has received and his experience. A rookie policeman cannot be expected to know as much as the senior sergeant, nor should he be held to the same standard of care. For this reason the statute provides a "reasonable officer" standard that includes experience and training. The result will be that different officers may receive different treatment for the same objective act, but this is fair. Because of the entity liability provisions, below, the victim-plaintiff does not suffer as a result.

Finally, there is the class of actions, taken by an officer who exercises due care, which still result in a constitutional deprivation. The victim still deserves compensation, of course, but there is no reason to hold the individual officer liable. He has measured up to the standard of behavior established for the "reasonable officer," and we should expect no more. Nor would a deterrent effect be forthcoming under these circumstances were sanctions imposed.

Perhaps the best example of behavior in this class is the enforcement of a law which the officer reasonably believes to be valid but which is later declared unconstitutional by a court of law. Particularly when the court's decision is a departure from established precedent, there is no reasonable way to expect the officer to predict the course of the law. His actions were exactly what would have been expected of a proper state official, and he should not be held liable. The proposal thus provides that, when an officer has acted neither intentionally nor negligently, he shall escape all liability under the Act for the constitutional deprivation suffered by the plaintiff.

Section 2.07 and 2.08 incorporate two widely recognized exceptions to tort liability into the new context. Legislators and judges, when acting in their official capacities, have been granted immunity at common law, and if the decisions of the United States Supreme Court are any indication,[8] the courts are not likely to accept incursion into these citadels even by the most unambiguous language. There are of course important reasons behind this immunity. Legislators and judges are expected to make choices in the course of their official activity, and the imposition of liability might well inhibit the freedom of choice otherwise encouraged by the law.

Having established the situations in which the individual officer will be subject to liability in damages under the Act, with the exception of punitive damages (which will be discussed below), we may turn our attention to the liability of the entity.

## WAIVER OF IMMUNITY (SECTION 3)

3.01—The State of _____ and all of its subdivisions, hereinafter referred to collectively as "entities," shall be subject to suit and liable in damages, as provided in this Act, for violations of constitutional rights of individuals. The defense of immunity, both as to suit and as to liability, is hereby expressly waived and shall not be asserted by the entity or its insurer in any cause of action arising under this Act. No distinction shall be made between governmental and proprietary activities of any entity to defeat liability under this Act.

## ENTITY LIABILITY (SECTION 4)

4.01—The entity shall be responsible for the satisfaction of the judgment, less the amount of officer liability, awarded for a constitutional violation committed by its officers acting under color of law.

4.02—The entity shall be responsible as guarantor of officer liability judgments. If the award against an officer-defendant shall not have been satisfied within ninety days from entry of final judgment, the plaintiff may notify the court of original jurisdiction of such fact under oath, and the court shall immediately upon receipt of such notification direct the entity to satisfy the amount of the judgment for which the officer is responsible within thirty days, provided however that if the entity shall have elected to satisfy the portion of the judgment for which it is directly responsible by payments at intervals under Sections 8.04–8.07 of this Act the amount still owing for officer liability shall be added to the remaining balance of entity liability. Failure to invoke this section within one year after the expiration of the ninety day period following entry of final judgment shall bar action by the plaintiff to require the entity to satisfy the officer-defendant's portion of the judgment.

4.03—No entity shall be held liable under the provisions of this Act for any deprivation of a constitutional right which shall occur as the result of the nondiscriminatory application of any statute, ordinance, rule, or other enactment duly passed by any legislative or quasi-legislative body unless the enactment shall first have been declared to be in violation of the Constitution of the United States, either on its face or as applied, by a court of competent jurisdiction in a declaratory or other proceeding.

4.04—The trial courts of general jurisdiction of this State shall have jurisdiction to hear claims of unconstitutionality of statutes, ordinances, rules, or other enactments of any legislative or quasi-legislative body in this state in actions for declaratory judgments.

The reason for the acceptance of the concept of governmental liability is preeminently practical. Unless the entity responsible for the officer is liable for the constitutional deprivation, the hope of finding a collectable defendant is slim indeed when the damages awarded are substantial. Our discussion of suits against the individual officer in Chapter 2 has already outlined the problems involved in suits against these officers alone, and if the proposed statute merely provided another remedy against judgment-proof defendants, it would hardly be worth the effort of presentation.

To achieve entity liability at all, the statute must waive immunity defenses previously available to governmental units in suits brought by private parties, and it must do so in clear and unmistakable terms. To avoid restrictive construction by the courts under the principle that statutes in derogation of the common law should be narrowly construed, the statute explicitly waives both immunity to suit and immunity to liability in damages. As further insurance against judicial emasculation, rejection of the governmental-proprietary distinction as a bar to liability has been made explicit. By these measures the legislative intent to take part in compensation of the victims of state-action constitutional violations should be made abundantly clear to even the most reluctant of courts.

By the provisions of Section 4.01, the statute makes explicit that the liability of the entity exists independently from that of the individual officer. The statute contemplates that damages awarded (the amount of which will be discussed below) are the responsiblity of the entity alone, with the exception of officer liability in limited amounts.[9]

As there were exceptions to individual-officer liability in earlier sections of the Act when circumstances warranted, so also there is an important exception to entity liability. Thus far we have been proceeding under at least the implicit assumption of a limited number of victims faced with a constitutional deprivation at the hands of a single officer. Raising the number of victims and the number of officers to several does not alter the picture seriously, but if the number of victims is raised to hundreds or thousands the fiscal implications for even the most fiscally sound entity become most serious. When such occurrences take place as the result of individual-officer action in a nonlegislative capacity, the proposed Act maintains the general standard of entity liability in whole or in part. It is assumed that by training and discipline the entity can reduce the risk of such behavior to an acceptable minimum.

The problem can arise in a different context, however. Constitutional deprivations may result from the good faith application of a statute or ordinance, and this application may affect hundreds or thousands of persons over time. To permit a finding of entity liability in this situation would be to invite financial disaster. For this reason Section 4.03 precludes entity liability for nondiscriminatory enforcement of a legislative or quasi-legislative enactment not previously declared unconstitutional by a court of competent jurisdiction.[10]

Fortunately, providing for protection against such financial disaster to the governmental treasury does not mean that the victim must be without a remedy. The statute provides for the issuance of a declaratory judgment against the validity of any statute or other legislative or quasi-legislative enactment in Section 4.04. In the event of defiance of the declaratory judgment, the entity becomes liable for punitive as well as compensatory damages.[11]

This solution is admittedly a trade-off. Past wrongs inflicted through the good faith enforcement of an unconstitutional statute will not be remedied under the terms of Section 4.03, but this is the price we must pay if we wish to avoid financial chaos for the entity. The provision for declaratory judgments, however, taken together with docket preference[12] provided later in the plan, limits the deprivations to a potentially minimal period. As soon as one person perceives a constitutional deprivation arising from the enforcement of a statute and brings suit under the Act, a ruling on the validity of the statute in question may be had. From the instant of a favorable judgment for the plaintiff, the entire range of damages under the Act becomes available if the tainted statute is again enforced.

There is a justification for the exception to entity liability carved out in Section 4.03 which goes beyond the problem of government finance. It is fully consistent with the normal doctrine that state legislative enactments carry a presumption of validity until a court of law determines to the contrary.

Before passing to a consideration of the types and amounts of damages, the words "other proceeding" in Section 4.03 deserve attention. The declaratory judgment remedy is not intended to be the exclusive device for testing statutory validity in the context of the proposed Act. Rather, it is included to offer an avenue of recourse for those victim-plaintiffs who otherwise would not have an opportunity to secure a judicial ruling on the constitutionality of the statute. For the private party already involved in a judicial dispute with the state the ruling of a court in that case would serve the same purpose, and once the statute or other legislative enactment has been declared unconstitutional by a court of competent jurisdiction in "a declaratory or other proceeding" the entity is on notice that the legislative enactment is no longer valid. Thus there are alternative routes to meeting the liability-producing standards set forth in Section 4.03, any one of which is sufficient to activate the liability provisions of the Act for enforcement of the statute in question.

## THE SCOPE OF DAMAGES (SECTION 5)

Having determined the basic distribution of liability between entity and officer, and by so doing having insured that a fiscally responsible defendant will be provided, let us now turn our attention to the types and amounts of damages to be awarded under the Act.

5.01—Damages under this Act shall be of three types: constitutional-compensatory, compensatory, and punitive.

5.02—Constitutional-compensatory damages shall be awarded for the deprivation of a constitutional right. A plaintiff prevailing in a cause of action arising under this Act shall be entitled to constitutional-compensatory damages of not less than one thousand dollars for each deprivation of a constitutional right as a matter of law. An award of constitutional-compensatory damages shall not exceed ten thousand dollars for any single deprivation.

5.03—Compensatory damages shall be awarded as in other civil actions, provided however that the amount shall not be less than the reasonable expenses incurred by the plaintiff as a result of the constitutional depriva- tion, including, but not limited to, medical expenses, investigatory costs in conjunction with the cause of action arising under this Act, and ex- penses incurred in the defense of any action, civil or criminal, commenced by an entity based wholly or in part on the fruits of a constitutional dep- rivation, provided however that such damages shall not be awarded for pain and suffering, mental anguish, or for attorney's fees in any cause of action arising under this Act. Nothing in this section shall be taken to exclude expenses not specifically enumerated herein from the class of ex- penses properly compensable under this Act in the absence of a specific exclusion.

5.04—Punitive damages shall be awarded in only two instances in causes of action arising under this Act:
(a) against entities, for enforcement of any statute, ordinance, or other enactment of any legislative or quasi-legislative body which previously has been declared unconstitutional, either on its face or as applied, as a matter of federal law by a court of competent jurisdiction; and
(b) against officers, for deprivations of constitutional rights resulting from intentional and willful action or from gross negligence and wanton disregard for the rights of the plaintiff.

5.05—Punitive damages shall be assessed in an amount consonant with the provisions of the law in other civil cases.

5.06—The methods and requirements for pleading damages shall be the same as in other civil cases.

One of the most serious shortcomings of the various remedial devices discussed above involved the lack of specific provision for recovery of damages for the deprivation of constitutional rights per se. Tort actions in the state courts, whether brought against the officer or against the entity, are framed in mostly common law terms and make no specific reference to damages which concern compensation for constitutional deprivations as such. The plaintiff bringing suit under the federal civil rights statute, 42 U.S.C. Section 1983, appeared to have been given the remedy we desire, but an examination of the cases led us to the conclusion that the federal courts consistently use the constitutional violation as a jurisdictional springboard and then proceed to decide the amount of damages on or- dinary tort grounds. If our statute is to be a significant improvement over existing remedies, it must make abundantly clear the intention to com- pensate for the constitutional deprivation, in and of itself, regardless of the extent of injuries compensable under other rubrics.

Closely related to the provision for damages for constitutional violations per se is the section dealing with the amount of damages to be allowed. Continuation of the practice, now permitted, by which the court or jury can return a verdict for the plaintiff but award only one cent or even absolutely nothing in the way of damages is unacceptable. By permitting such miscarriages of justice, the law proclaims that the federal constitutional rights of at least some persons are indeed worthless. To avoid this possibility, the proposed statute establishes a minimum amount which must be awarded to the plaintiff upon a finding in his favor on the matter of a constitutional deprivation, whether or not he sustained any out-of-pocket expenses worthy of compensation.

The need for minimum damages is obvious, but a more difficult question arises when we face the amount of such damages. It may be argued that to place a dollar value on constitutional rights is to cheapen them because, after all, these rights are in one sense priceless. True as it may be that these rights are not up for purchase at any price, the argument carries with it its opposite as a practical consequence. By refusing to set a dollar value, at least as a minimum, on these admittedly most precious rights, we permit the American legal system in effect to pronounce them worthless. The noble sentiment leads to a most base result. To this writer, at least, it seems far preferable to guarantee something in the way of compensation than to stand on so high a pedestal and permit nothing. After all, the victim-plaintiff is not attempting to sell his birthright. He will retain his federal constitutional rights in the future. What he is doing is simply attempting to secure compensation for a past violation.

It is conceded that the scale established in the Act for constitutional-compensatory damages is an arbitrary one, but any amount will be arbitrary. The minimum amount is set at one thousand dollars. Should those hoping to adopt legislation of the type proposed feel that the amount is too low, nothing stands in the way of raising the minimum award. Nothing stands in the way of lowering it, either, but more care should be employed in this direction lest the amount be made so low as to indicate a lack of respect for the constitutional rights involved.

A provision of the statute somewhat more likely to be controversial is the proposed maximum amount that can be allowed for any single constitutional deprivation per se. This provision is designed primarily to make the legislative package acceptable in practical budgetary terms. As will be discussed below in the section on insurance coverage, uncertainty as to the amount of potential liability can make insurance impossible to obtain. If insurance cannot be purchased at a reasonable price, and if potentially limitless awards are paraded before the eyes of legislators considering the bill containing the remedies proposed here, the chances for passage into law may well be minimal. A legislator would not be deserving of blame for refusing to vote for the adoption of a plan for entity liability that offered the very real possibility of entity-crippling judgments against which no insurance could be secured at any price within reason. Once again we are faced with the question of whether the achievement of a substantial recovery for a constitutional deprivation per se is worth making concessions to practicality, and once again the answer is in the affirmative. Thus, the provisions of the model bill set a $10,000 maximum recovery for each constitutional deprivation per se.

Within the range thus created (between one and ten thousand dollars), the court or jury would be left to its sound discretion in setting the exact dollar amount. In this fashion the "conscience of the community" is allowed to operate, but only within a clearly specified range. In this fashion the court may make awards for harassment, aggravated deprivations, and the like, which no statute could specify with sufficient clarity to meet all future situations.

In addition to the damages for the constitutional violation per se, many victim-plaintiffs will be entitled to compensation for out-of-pocket expenses in the same manner as in an ordinary tort action. No novel doctrines are required for this provision of the Act, and the experience of the American jurisdictions which have adopted governmental tort liability should allay any fears of the state going bankrupt from tort claims. The Act allows, first of all, recovery for medical bills and investigation costs related to the plaintiff's suit under the new law.

Beyond these expenses, the Act allows recovery of expenses (including attorney's fees) incurred in any suit instituted by an entity based wholly or partially on the fruits of a constitutional deprivation. This provision is designed to prevent the impoverishment of a victim by the defense of one or more suits as the result of unconstitutional state action. The mere exclusion of the "fruits of the poisonous tree" from evidence in a criminal proceeding is insufficient to make the victim whole. The costs incurred for the picking and using of the fruits must inevitably fall upon either the victim or the entity, and this scheme opts for the victim's full compensation for any expenses visited upon him as an outgrowth of an entity's unconstitutional action.[13]

Damages in the way of lost income and the like (usually styled "special damages") will be subject to the specific pleading requirements of the state's laws.

One exception to the ordinary run of compensatory damages has been included in the Act. Awards for "pain and suffering" have been excluded. This "wild card" of tort litigation has accounted for astronomical judgments in private suits, and, were it to be included in the statute, the same factors motivating legislative rejection of the entire package noted above concerning unlimited awards for constitutional deprivations per se would be allowed to reappear.

Punitive damages against an entity are allowed only in narrowly circumscribed instances. Ordinarily, punitive damages may not be recovered against entities even in those jurisdictions which have abrogated sovereign immunity,[14] and our scheme is designed to be compensatory rather than punitive. In one situation, however, an exception will be made in the hope that a deterrent effect will be forthcoming. In the event that a plaintiff has secured a declaratory judgment (or other judicial ruling) against the enforcement of a legislative or quasi-legislative enactment on constitutional grounds and the entity proceeds to enforce the enactment in defiance of the court's ruling, there appears to be sufficient cause to provide for punitive damages against the entity as an example to other governmental units which might be tempted to follow suit.

In the case of the individual officer, punitive damages conform more closely to the ordinary practice in tort law. In the case of intentional deprivations of constitutional rights (in the "specific intent" sense) or of gross negligence and wanton disregard for the rights of the plaintiff, the court is permitted to award punitive damages.

It is submitted that these provisions of the Act will overcome one of the most glaring failures of the presently existing remedies. No longer will a plaintiff receive a verdict and a one cent award. Provision for specific damages for the constitutional deprivation per se also avoids the current possibility of its being bypassed in the consideration of damages—which turn out to be based on ordinary tort principles of compensation for out-of-pocket losses. Yet with these added benefits for the victim-plaintiff, the Act proposed here is not one which threatens to bankrupt the entity-defendant.[15] By limiting the maximum recovery for constitutional violations per se, by prohibiting pain and suffering awards, and by strictly limiting punitive damages against an entity, governmental units should be able to calculate their potential liability by considering ordinary tort liability experiences in those states where sovereign immunity has been abolished. Likewise, providers of insurance coverage for the entities should have adequate information on which to formulate their rates.

## THE PAYMENT OF INTEREST (SECTION 6)

When a victim-plaintiff has suffered out-of-pocket expenses as a result of his constitutional deprivation he has been deprived of the opportunity to use those funds for other purposes, including, but not limited to, investment or savings. For this reason, the plan provides that interest shall accrue from the date of such expenditures or losses at a rate found reasonable by the court.

6.01—Interest shall accrue on all compensatory and constitutional-compensatory damages under the provisions of this Act at a reasonable rate to be determined by the court and shall be assessed from the date of actual expenditure or loss until satisfaction of the judgment.

This provision serves two purposes. First, it protects the financial interests of the plaintiff-victim. Second, it acts as an incentive for the defendants to bring the issue to trial as soon as they are ready. Unnecessary delay simply results in a larger expenditure than would have been necessary had the defendants proceeded to trial promptly.[16]

## PROVIDING FOR REMEDIES BEYOND COMPENSATION (SECTION 7)

7.01—If the victim of a constitutional deprivation actionable under the provisions of this Act shall have been made the subject of any official record or report which may reflect negatively upon said victim as a result of action initiated by any entity or officer based in whole or in part on the fruits of the constitutional deprivation, the court shall at the plaintiff's request order such report or record expunged.

7.02—In all proceedings subject to the laws of this state, whether public or private, the plaintiff who has successfully invoked Section 7.01 of this Act shall be entitled to deny that records ordered expunged have ever existed, and no entity or officer shall make known, or cause to be made known, any information to the contrary following the order of the court. No criminal or civil liability shall ever attach for the invocation of the provisions of this section.

7.03—Courts having jurisdiction to hear causes of action arising under this Act shall be authorized to fashion such additional remedies against entities and officers as shall be necessary to constitute a complete and adequate remedy.

Some constitutional deprivations will result in the victim's arrest. Even if he is eventually acquitted, the arrest record will remain to haunt him for the rest of his days when he seeks employment, applies for insurance of certain types, seeks a security clearance, and in other situations as well. To be truly remedial, the proposed Act must also undo these extra-legal outgrowths of the deprivations to the maximum extent possible. For this reason the statute specifically provides for the expunging of official records made by the state or its subdivisions as a result of the deprivation.[17] Beyond the expunging itself the Act explicitly allows the victim to deny that the records ever existed and prohibits any legal actions against him for such denials.

Finally, the Act provides an "elastic clause" to provide for remedial action by the court when money damages and clearing of official records alone would be insufficient to secure a complete and adequate remedy. Relief granted under this section might normally be expected to be of the equitable variety.

## PAYMENT TO THE VICTIM (SECTION 8)

8.01—Unless an entity shall elect to satisfy a judgment entered under the provisions of this Act at intervals as provided in Sections 8.04–8.07, it shall pay in full that portion of the judgment for which it is directly responsible within thirty days from the entry of final judgment.

8.02—Payment shall be made by certified check to the plaintiff at his address of record, provided however, that if such address is unknown said payment shall be made to the attorney of record for the plaintiff at said attorney's place of business.

8.03—Transmittal of the certified check required in Section 8.02 shall be by registered mail.

8.04—Defendant entities in causes of action arising under this Act may elect to satisfy judgments for which they are responsible either directly or as guarantor by payments at intervals to be established with the approval of the court, provided however that the intervals shall not exceed one year between payments and that the total period of payment shall not exceed ten years from a date thirty days after the entry of final judgment.

8.05—Judgments satisfied by payments at intervals under Section 8.04 shall be subject to interest, payable to the plaintiff, at a reasonable rate to be determined by the court.

8.06—An entity may pay any portion or the total amount of the judgment in advance of the schedule established under Section 8.04.

8.07—The interest provided for in Section 8.05 shall be in addition to any other interest found due under other provisions of this Act.

8.08—The provisions of Sections 8.04–8.07 shall be inapplicable to that portion of the judgment which shall be satisifed by an insurer of the entity.

In those cases in which the plaintiff prevails under the Act the statute must provide for prompt satisfaction of the judgment. In the ordinary case the proposal permits thirty days for the payment of the total award. The situation may arise, however, in which the entity cannot meet the judgment from its immediately available funds. In the case of an ordinary tort judgment, the judgment-creditor could levy on the property of the judgment-debtor and secure payment from the sale of that property, but in the case of an entity this frequently would mean the taking of property involved in vital public services. It would be unwise to force the sale of the county courthouse, or the county hospital, to satisfy the judgment if other means are available which provide a reasonable alternative. To deprive the citizens served by the entity of essential governmental services without overwhelming justification would be an excessive price to pay.

In order to avoid unnecessary hardship on the citizens of the entity while at the same time protecting the interests of the victim-plaintiff the Act provides for installment payments in satisfaction of the judgment against an entity in those cases in which the entity desires to spread the payments over a span of years.

Interest, at a reasonable rate to be determined by the court, will be charged on the unpaid portion of the judgment. This protects the financial interests of the plaintiff and at the same time should serve as an incentive to the entity to satisfy the judgment in the shortest feasible time.

Section 8.08 is inserted to prevent an insurance company from taking advantage of the payment-at-intervals provision, which was inserted for the sole purpose of preventing the disruption of necessary governmental services by judgments awarded under the provisions of the proposed Act.

## THE COST OF COUNSEL (SECTION 9)

9.01—In all causes of action arising under this Act the prevailing plaintiff's counsel of record shall be entitled to an award of reasonable fees in an amount set by the court, which shall be taxed against the defendant entity and which shall in no instance be less than twenty-five percent of the amount awarded in damages, provided however that if counsel shall demonstrate to the satisfaction of the court that his customary fee in actions similar to those arising under this Act is greater than the minimum fee herein specified he shall be awarded the greater amount.

9.02—Attorney fees awarded under this section shall be in addition to the amount awarded in damages to the plaintiff.

9.03—In suits for declaratory judgments against an entity under the provisions of section 4.04 counsel of record for the prevailing plaintiff shall be awarded reasonable fees by the court, provided that the fees awarded shall not be less than the amount customarily received by said counsel in declaratory judgment actions, or than the amount customary in the jurisdiction in which the action was tried in the event that the customary fees of counsel cannot be demonstrated to the satisfaction of the court.

In the realm of criminal law American courts have recognized that an individual defendant without assistance of adequate legal counsel is at the mercy of the state. This proposition is equally true when it is the private citizen who is the plaintiff in an action against the state. Particularly in an area as complex as the adjudication of constitutional rights, the layman without adequate counsel will be greatly disadvantaged in an attempt to secure a true test of the merits of his claim. We must, therefore, consider how most adequately to assure that the aggrieved citizen can secure that assistance.

The word "adequate" should be stressed in the context of assistance of counsel. It is not enough in any realistic sense to say that a scheme will allow the plaintiff to secure an attorney. He must be able to secure an attorney skilled and knowledgeable in what will no doubt become a highly specialized area of the law—constitutional damage claims.

As with many other fields of endeavor, the law has become far too broad in this day and age for any one lawyer to be fully competent in all areas of practice, and the state government will be among the first to recognize this fact and act accordingly. It is safe to predict that a natural consequence of adoption of the proposed Act will be the creation of special sections in the offices of the state Attorney General and of the local entities' legal divisions to deal with the claims which will be forthcoming. The personnel of these sections will, over time, develop the expertise which comes from immersion in this area of state law. By constant contact with the latest developments and by practical experience (the "feel" for the area) in preparation and trial of cases, the state's specialized attorneys will become highly skilled in defending the treasury against constitutional deprivation damage suits. Thus far no problems arise —it is surely in the interest of justice that the state be represented by highly skilled counsel who can act vigorously to protect it from invalid claims.

It is also true, however, that justice is not served when the two sides to a legal controversy are mismatched. Just as it is in the interests of justice to have top-flight lawyers for the state, so is it also in the interest of justice to have excellent counsel at the plaintiff's table. To provide a "fair fight" in the adversary setting of American law, then, we must make available to the plaintiff counsel who are equal to the task—attorneys who have achieved a level of expertise equal to that possessed by the counsel for the government.

There would seem to be two potential barriers to fulfilling this need— one absolute and the other relative. First, it is possible that the rewards of such practice might be so low as to attract no one to specialize on the plaintiff's side of such litigation (or to attract only those with less than outstanding ability). This would mean that no adequate counsel would in fact be available. A more likely possibility is that there would be some excellent counsel available—at a premium price—which in turn might mean that their availability would depend on the financial resources of the victim-plaintiff.[18]

Both of these potential barriers rest on the same foundation—money.[19] It is reasonable to expect that there will be an adequate supply of counsel for the plaintiff only if there are sufficient economic rewards for such specialization. How, then, can this be provided? Two potential sources for attorney's fees can be found in American law. The first is the plaintiff, and the second is the defendant.

The plaintiff can be the source of legal fees for counsel on either a contingent fee basis (receiving a given percentage of the award) or on a flat fee arrangement. In the ordinary course of tort litigation the preference for the contingent fee is simply explained. The prospective plaintiff is more willing to litigate when he knows he will not have to pay a sizable legal fee if he loses the case.

The flat fee arrangement (where a definite amount is established by agreement or by law) has obvious drawbacks in our situation. First, many potential litigants might be dissuaded from asserting valid claims by the fear that they might be worse off at the end of the litigation than when they started. Second, a flat fee would have to be set relatively high in order to attract competent counsel, and in the event of a small judgment the fee might well surpass the award, again leaving the plaintiff worse off than when he started the litigation.

The contingent fee, on the other hand, apparently meets these problems. There seems to be no dearth of private tort actions because of legal fee problems. The prospective plaintiff is not deterred by the fear of the size of the lawyer's bill at the end of an unsuccessful law suit, and if the award is small he knows that his attorney's fees will likewise be minimal.

In the realm of the contingent fee, there appears to be a range along which fees may run stretching between the wide-open situation of total freedom of lawyer and client to bargain over the percentage[20] to the situation in which the amount of the contingent fee is regulated by statutory provision setting a maximum (and possibly a minimum) limit. At the "open" end of the spectrum the plaintiff runs the risk of being required to pay a very substantial portion of his award (which for the most part is supposed to be compensatory)—frequently up to 50%—to his lawyer. At the other end of the scale, a legislatively set maximum rate may be so low as to act as an impediment to the acceptance of such cases by the most qualified attorneys. This is indeed the case under the Federal Tort Claims Act. Wright's study[21] found that many firms were unwilling to handle Federal Tort Claims Act cases simply because of the fee limitation written into the statute by Congress. The legislative aim (to protect the plaintiff from the possibility of losing most of his award in fees)[22] may be a noble one, but the device employed is sadly inappropriate if it deprives him of an essential tool for any recovery. Wright's suggestion for solving the problem of counsel unavailability is simple. Remove the fee limitation, and let the plaintiff bargain for the best attorney he can find. Unfortunately, the plaintiff may not find much left in his pocket under the Wright "solution."

It thus appears that both the Wright solution and the congressional solution may mean the same thing for the victim-plaintiff—receipt of less than the amount necessary to make him "whole" again (or as nearly so as possible through the use of money damages) after a deprivation of his constitutional rights by state action. No matter how the pie is sliced, so long as the fees come from the plaintiff his judgment is not going to be 100% compensatory insofar as his financial position is concerned. If we are indeed committed to compensating the victim in full measure, he must be the sole beneficiary of any award of damages.[23]

The alternative is for the defendant to be the source of the fees for the plaintiff's attorney. The two most likely variations here would be for the entity[24] to pay the fees in all cases brought under the Act (whether or not the plaintiff prevailed) or for the entity to pay attorney's fees only when the plaintiff's action is successful. The first possibility is unacceptable for several reasons. First, it would be likely to encourage nuisance litigation. There would be no financial deterrent to counsel or client should they wish to push any far-fetched claim at the resulting expense of the public treasury for the defense of the case. While it is of course necessary to attempt to prevent borderline cases from being barred from trial by practical monetary considerations, the remedy of paying for all cases regardless of merit is too drastic. Beyond the cost to the public in direct defense of such nuisance suits, and the possible costs of monetary settlements to avoid trial, there is the additional burden on already overcrowded dockets in the state courts.[25]

Further, the amount of the fees would be a problem if the plaintiff lost the case. The fixed fee solution would still have the problems set out above, and of course there would be no award against which to measure contingent fees. One can easily imagine the problems of using a standard such as that of the damages claimed by the plaintiff in his complaint to measure the attorney's fees. If we may assume that counsel will be willing to handle most of the meritorious claims on a contingent fee basis, it seems that entity payment of fees—the second possibility—only in those cases in which the plaintiff prevails is a preferable solution.

The major problem to be solved in the contingent fee arrangement is that of providing an adequate fee without the entity finding itself subject to excessive charges. Again we have the continuum of possible fee arrangements. Here, however, the "open-ended" agreement between plaintiff and counsel makes no sense. Neither would have any interest in holding the fee down. Nor does it make sense to consider the state and the plaintiff's counsel negotiating on the fee. The situation simply does not conform to a "negotiated" type of contingent fee.

We have already eliminated one portion of the flat fee (that in situations where the plaintiff loses his case), but it is still conceivable that the Act might provide a flat fee in those cases in which the plaintiff prevails. Here we once again face the problem of attracting competent counsel without making the fee so high as to be improper in small cases.[26]

The percentage contingent fee set by statute is another possibility, but the disadvantages discussed above apply with equal weight in a situation in which the entity pays. The position of counsel is exactly the same regardless of the source of his fee, and the same dangers lurk. Of course the legislature would not be motivated to set the fee at a low level to protect the plaintiff's award, but an equally compelling motive (at least in the legislative mind) could be to protect the treasury.[27]

The solution to the problem adopted in the proposed Act is to allow the court to determine reasonable fees in each case, and in this determination several factors are worthy of consideration. First, a relevant factor is the "going rate" in private damage actions. If lawyers are to be available for our prospective plaintiffs, they should not be expected to take a financial loss every time they accept a case against an entity on a constitutional deprivation issue, and the logical starting point is to look at the fees charged by the attorney if he were involved in private tort litigation (unless he specializes in constitutional rights cases against entities).

The question then arises as to what the standard should be within this criterion. Should the relevant measurement be the statewide average for such fees, the rate prevailing in the local jurisdiction, or the rate usually charged by the particular attorney? In light of our objective of securing highly qualified counsel for the plaintiff, the most desirable standard is the third. If there were to be significant differences between the fees an outstanding lawyer receives in different parts of the state, he might well be discouraged from taking cases in the lower-paying regions. Likewise, a statewide average standard would discourage the acceptance of cases by out-of-state counsel in those instances where the state's average was low when compared to other states'.

The discussion to this point has been based on the assumption that the plaintiff has sought and recovered an award of money damages under the Act. One provision of the statute is not amenable to such interpretation. Section 4.04 provides for declaratory judgments in favor of the plaintiff.

In this type of proceeding there cannot be a fee contingent on an award of damages. For the reasons already set out it seems unwise to attempt a flat fee arrangement. Rather, the proposed statute leaves the question of the appropriate fee to the sound discretion of the court, with the proviso that the attorney's customary fee for delcaratory judgment suits shall be the minimum reasonable fee (or, if such a standard is lacking, the average fee in the jurisdiction shall be the minimum).

The mechanics of the process should be such as to insure prompt and direct payment of fees to the attorney. Because the fee is not part of the plaintiff's award, there is no reason to funnel the funds through him, and the potential problem of his failure to pay his attorney should be eliminated. The following section is designed to accomplish these ends:

9.04—Payment of attorney fees awarded under this Act shall be made directly to the attorney of record for the plaintiff within thirty days of the entry of final judgment, unless the entity shall elect to satisfy the judgment by payments at intervals as provided in Sections 8.04–8.07 of this Act, in which case the attorney fees shall be paid in a like manner and with like interest.

The clause in the proposed Section 9.04 concerning payment at intervals is designed to guarantee that the plaintiff does not take second place to counsel in order of payment if the entity is unable to pay both the award and the fees immediately. The plan is designed first and foremost to protect the individual victim-plaintiff and not to guarantee a lawyer's income to the detriment of the interests of his client. On the other hand, the attorney should not be forced to wait until the entire judgment has been satisfied before he sees the first cent of his fee. An equitable arrangement is proportional payment to both plaintiff and counsel under the same installment mechanism. This procedure will also have the additional benefit of maintaining the attorney's interest in prompt payment of the installments due his client.

The final sections of the proposed Act which concern the fees to be paid to counsel are designed to protect the victim-plaintiff from the small minority of unscrupulous attorneys who would attempt to secure additional payments from their clients.

9.05—No attorney shall request or receive, from the plaintiff in any cause of action arising under this Act or from any other source, any fee or other compensation for his services not provided for in Sections 9.01–9.04. Violation of this section shall be a misdemeanor punishable by forfeiture of both the properly awarded attorney's fees and the amounts collected in violation of this section. In addition, any person found guilty of violating this section shall be fined not less than five hundred dollars nor more than one thousand dollars for each offense and may be imprisoned for a term not to exceed one year for each offense.

9.06—Fees forfeited under Section 9.05 shall be returned to the treasurer or other appropriate officer of the entity against which they were taxed, and amounts received in violation of Section 9.05 shall be returned to the party who shall have paid them, provided that if the identity of said party cannot be determined the amount forfeited shall likewise be paid over to the treasurer or other appropriate officer of the entity against which attorney's fees were taxed. All sums collected as fines shall be disposed of as otherwise provided by the laws of this state.

These provisions, then, are designed to assure the victim of a constitutional deprivation at the hands of a state officer that the remedy provided in the Act will be readily available and that there will be no hidden charges foisted upon him by a less than honest attorney.

Taken as a whole, Section 9 of the proposed statute is structured to avoid the problem found in the Federal Tort Claims Act. The provisions should make adequate counsel readily available to victims of constitutional deprivations, and the criminal provisions should further protect the plaintiff from the (hopefully rare) possibility of the corrupt attorney who would attempt to fatten his purse with the funds of the plaintiff in addition to the fees awarded him under the statute.

## LIMITATION ON ASSESSMENT OF COURT COSTS (SECTION 10)

10.01—In causes of action arising under this Act costs shall not be assessed against the plaintiff, provided however that this section shall be inapplicable if the court shall find that the claim asserted by the plaintiff is frivolous and totally without legal merit.

The prospect of being saddled with court costs in the event of an unsuccessful suit may be sufficient to deter many a plaintiff from asserting his rights under the Act. Therefore it is proposed that, in the ordinary case of a good faith suit, no costs be assessed against the plaintiff even if he loses the case. To avoid nuisance suits, however, the court is given the discretion of assessing costs if it determines that the plaintiff's position is entirely frivolous.

## THE FORUM AND THE VENUE (SECTION 11)

11.01—Original jurisdiction in causes of action arising under this Act shall be in the trial courts of general jurisdiction of this state. Appellate jurisdiction shall be the same as provided by statute for other civil actions.

11.02—Venue shall be in the court of general jurisdiction for the county in which the plaintiff resides, in which the deprivation is alleged to have occurred, or in which the entity shall have its principal office, at the election of the plaintiff.

11.03—Changes of venue shall be taken as in other civil actions.

11.04—In those courts which shall sit in divisions, the presiding judge may designate one or more divisions to hear all causes of action arising under this Act, subject to the provisions of Section 14.

Consideration of the appropriate forum for the determination of constitutional deprivations claims raises the question of whether it is more appropriate for the cause to be heard in the ordinary trial courts of the state or in a specialized tribunal such as a court of claims.[28] There is much to be said for a specialized court in terms of building expertise among its members and developing a consistent body of rulings, but ordinarily such specialized courts are located only in the principal cities of a state (or possibly only in the state capital). Although data are lacking on the issue of travel to a distant forum as a deterrent to suit, two factors are at least initially plausible. First, the costs of such travel and the costs of accommodations during an extended trial could act to discourage litigation. The plaintiff might escape his attorney's fees if he lost the case by making a contingent fee arrangement (even if the provisions in Section 9 were not adopted), but the potentially sizeable expenses for travel to a distant forum would remain. Particularly for the less-than-affluent victim-plaintiff, these expenses could make recovery a practical impossibility because of the very real inability to take the financial risk of making the journey to a distant forum.

A second potential inhibiting factor would arise among those elements of society whose "world" amounts to a neighborhood or ghetto. Unfamiliar with other surroundings and unable to cope with the threat of a strange environment, they might decline to leave their own little world. Once again, the distance of the forum could act as a practical bar to recovery.

On the other hand, use of the regular trial courts of the state will mean that the forum will be located within easy reach of most victim-plaintiffs. Trial courts of general jurisdiction are normally located in each county and thus would be within a relatively short distance from the home of the plaintiff.

The consistency of rulings hoped for from the specialized court would of course be lost, but it is possible that there will be a trade-off advantage. As Hink and Schutter have noted,[29] use of the general trial courts automatically makes appeal to higher courts available. Appellate review of the decisions of specialized courts is frequently quite limited.

Some specialization could be obtained, even within the general framework suggested here, in jurisdictions within the state which have multi-judge courts. All constitutional-damage actions may be assigned to a particular division or judge. For the rest of the desired consistency, the proposed Act relies upon the same method available in other civil proceedings—correction of improper trial court rulings by appellate decision.

The location of the trial is also a matter of concern to the potential plaintiff. It has been noted above, in the discussion of the federal damage remedy against individual officers under 42 U.S.C. Section 1983, that it can be an advantage to have the trial held at a location somewhat removed form that of the officer's residence to avoid local pressures. In the case of entity liability, similar factors might well be present, particularly in a small community in which "outsiders" are looked upon with suspicion and in which a nonresident plaintiff is seeking an award of damages of sufficient size to bring about a direct and immediate increase in the taxes of the residents of the community.

To compensate for this danger, provision is made in the Act for alternative venues for trial. The first option is the jurisdiction in which the plaintiff resides. The second venue is the jurisdiction in which the consitutional deprivation is alleged to have taken place. In many instances, these two options will in actuality be one because it seems likely that many deprivations will occur in and around the home of the victim-plaintiff. In some instances, however, the second-venue option might be of advantage to the victim who was away from his place of residence when the deprivation took place. Finally, an option is provided for the suit to be tried in jurisdiction in which the entity maintains its general office. When the state is a party, this provision gives the option of trying the case in the state capital. This opens the possibility, at least, of more specialization than otherwise could occur, but it does not do so in a way which forces the plaintiff to make the journey to the state capital against his will.

For those cases in which the local citizenry is so inflamed against a particular plaintiff that he cannot receive a fair trial or in which there are other reasons which would ordinarily call for a change of venue in civil actions, the Act provides that the ordinary civil change of venue rules shall apply.

It is hoped that the provisions of Section 11 will provide a convenient forum for the victim-plaintiff. If this goal is reached, and if the plaintiff is spared the burden of travel to a distant forum, another step will have been taken toward making the remedies offered by the statute truly available to all rather than their being only distant possibilities dimly perceived.

PROCEDURAL MATTERS AND EVIDENTIARY RULES (SECTION 12)

12.01—Unless otherwise provided in this Act, the rules of procedure and evidence generally applicable in civil proceedings shall apply in causes of action arising under this Act.

12.02—Evidence or testimony concerning criminal charges or proceedings against the plaintiff in a cause of action arising under this Act which have been determined by a court of competent jurisdiction to have been based in whole or in part upon the fruits of a constitutional deprivation alleged by the plaintiff in a cause of action arising under this Act shall be inadmissible in said cause of action, provided however that the resolution of the constitutional claims in favor of the defendant in said criminal action shall be admissible at the discretion of the plaintiff in proceedings under this Act.

One shortcoming mentioned in the discussion of existing remedies was that when the plaintiff could be shown to be of low "status," his chances of recovering substantial money damages were, as a matter of practical reality, very small indeed. Part of this problem has already been removed by not allowing damages for pain and suffering. The plaintiff cannot plead damage to reputation, and the defense cannot undermine his entire case by showing his status to be so low as not to be entitled to damages for loss of reputation.

A second factor to be removed from consideration is the post-violation fate of the plaintiff. Operating on the premise that constitutional rights are available equally to all, we conclude that a subsequent criminal conviction should not be allowed to decrease the plaintiff's chances for recovery.

To prevent "inadvertent" slips by witnesses for the entity which might operate to poison the atmosphere of the trial, the following "incentives" to proper behavior are included:

12.03—Statements made in the presence of the court or jury, or actions taken in the presence of the court or jury, which shall have the effect of making known information which would be precluded by Section 12.02 shall be grounds for a mistrial at the option of the plaintiff.

12.04—Willful violation of sections 12.02-12.03 shall be a misdemeanor punishable by a fine not to exceed five hundred dollars, and shall further result in civil liability in the same manner as a constitutional deprivation under this Act, provided that said civil liability shall not be less than two hundred fifty nor more than five hundred dollars.

THE USE OF A JURY (SECTION 13)

13.01—Trial by jury is preserved in causes of action arising under this Act, provided however that a jury may be waived by consent of all parties to the action.

While the general practice in claims actions against governmental entities has been to require trial to the court alone without a jury, this alternative is rejected in the proposed statute. The principal reason advanced for the abolition of jury trial, the fear of excessive awards, has been rendered unpersuasive by the limits of liability written into the statute concerning entities. Furthermore, it may be that the individual officer defendant is entitled to a jury trial as a matter of his constitutional rights under the Seventh Amendment. It might be argued that the action contemplated in the statute is not a "suit at common law" because such hybrid entity-officer liability was unknown at common law, but the spirit of the Amendment would be violated, if not the letter, by denying the defendant officer a jury trial, particularly when the action is expressly intended to replace the common law tort remedies against the individual officer.[30]

## SPEEDING THE TRIAL: DOCKET PLACEMENT (SECTION 14)

14.01—Causes of action arising under this Act shall be given docket preference over all other civil actions with the exception of challenges to election returns.

14.02—Suits for declaratory relief under this Act shall have docket preference over suits for money damages under this Act.

14.03—In those jurisdictions in which the presiding judge has designated one or more judges or divisions of the court to hear all causes of action arising under this Act, pursuant to the provisions of Section 11.04, the docket preference herein provided shall be inapplicable in all other divisions, or in cases before other judges, provided however that if a cause shall not have been heard within one hundred eighty days after its filing the presiding judgge shall transfer said cause of action to another division or judge on motion of any party and the docket preference provided in Sections 14.01–14.02 shall apply.

Cases involving constitutional rights deserve the highest priority in the courts of the state. In these days of crowded dockets and delays running into months and even years, it would be incongruous indeed to establish what appears to be a liberal statutory plan for remedies only to have the plaintiffs languish in the shadows cast by suits over automobile accidents, alienation of affection, ordinary trespass, and other purely private legal conflicts. The supremacy clause of the Constitution gives the provisions of that document favored treatment over statutes and constitutions of the states, and it is not unreasonable to provide that those persons asserting fundamental rights under the Constitution should have docket preference over those asserting rights arising under common law or state law.

In addition, the provisions for interest on the judgment contained in Section 6 will mean that extended delay will cause further amounts to be extracted from the public treasury. Docket preference will thus also work to lessen the financial burden on the entity and the officer (if he is personally liable).

The one exception to this docket preference is for election contests which traditionally have been granted docket preference and which go to the very heart of proper governmental operation.

In those jurisdictions with trial courts divided into divisions it is hoped that specialization will occur in the area of suits for constitutional damages. To encourage this specialization, the docket preference provision is not generally applicable to all divisions of such courts. However, if the specialized division becomes overloaded with cases the Act provides for the shifting of delayed cases to other divisions of the court with docket preference being reinstated.

## PREVENTING MULTIPLE SUITS BY A SINGLE PLAINTIFF (SECTION 15)

15.01—Institution of an action under the provisions of this Act shall bar any other civil remedy sought by the same plaintiff against the same defendant-entity or -officer for damages arising out of the same act or occurrence. Institution of an action in the courts of this State or of the United States for damages arising out of an act or occurrence which would otherwise give rise to a cause of action under this Act shall bar any suit or recovery under this Act.

The victim-plaintiff is provided with a comprehensive remedy under the proposed Act, both for his constitutional deprivation per se and for compensation which ordinarily would be recovered in a tort proceeding against the officer (or against the entity in those states in which such suits are permitted). He should not be allowed to attempt to recover again under those other statutory and common law remedial mechanisms, nor should the defendant entity or officer be subjected to the expense of defending another action. Therefore the plan provides that the plaintiff's election to proceed under the proposed Act shall bar suits under other provisions of state law.[31] Further provision is made to prevent the reverse attempt. Institution of an action against a defendant officer in a federal civil rights remedy proceeding or against an officer or entity in any state civil proceeding is made a complete bar to suit under the provisions of the Act.

Beyond the desire to prevent a plaintiff from recovering twice over for the same loss there is the practical motivation of making the plan more palatable to the state legislature. Except for the culprit who goes about intentionally violating constitutional rights, the position of the individual officer will be much improved under the Act. Instead of being open to liability (at least theoretically) for large amounts, he will be subject only to strictly limited liability. This is an improvement in the legal position of the officer, and one might well expect state and local governmental employees' associations to support such a package in the state legislature if they were aware of the advantages.[32] If, as has been suggested, one of the reasons for the slow progress in tort liability waiver by the states (through legislative action) is the lack of organized interest-group pressure,[33] the plan proposed here might fare somewhat better in the legislative arena. Even though the officers may not be sued frequently as individuals under present law, they often are required to have personal performance bonds. It is submitted that sharply decreased potential liability for the individual officer would lead to a corresponding decrease in the cost of bonding (and of insurance), and once again the interest groups oriented toward state employees are not likely to overlook this benefit to their members.

### SETTLING OUT OF COURT (SECTION 16)

16.01—Nothing in this Act shall operate to bar informal settlement of claims arising hereunder in a manner consistent with the provisions of Sections 16.02–16.03.

16.02—No settlement shall be for an amount less than the minimum amount established by law for the constitutional-compensatory damages claimed plus the actual out-of-pocket expenses alleged.

16.03—No settlement shall be made without the approval of the court having jurisdiction over the cause of action.

The provisions of Section 16 are designed to permit settlement of claims before a case comes to trial, but they are written to provide protection for the litigant and the defendants. First, they prevent an entity from settling for an amount that is only a fraction of its true potential liability. In the instances of a valid claim by the plaintiff, the section works to his advantage. In those instances in which the plaintiff's case is a weak one it is conceivable that in dollars-and-cents terms, this section could work to his disadvantage in that he will receive nothing at trial and might have secured a minimal settlement from the entity which desired to avoid the costs of litigation; but the purpose of the Act is not to guarantee payment on all claims no matter how weak. It is to guarantee a full hearing before a court of law on the constitutional deprivation allegation and, if the plaintiff prevails, to guarantee a truly compensatory award which can be collected.

Second, the provisions of Section 16 should serve as a deterrent to excessive claims by the plaintiff, at least when his attorney wishes to reach a settlement before trial. An excessive claim for out-of-pocket damages cannot be "negotiated" in the settlement process under the statute. Also, by prohibiting the settlement of "nuisance" suits for a small amount (because of the minimal damages established for constitutional deprivations per se), the Act should operate as a deterrent to the filing of such suits.

## AUTHORIZATION FOR THE PURCHASE OF INSURANCE (SECTION 17)

17.01—Entities are hereby authorized to purchase insurance for part or all of their liability for constitutional deprivations.

The entities which are potentially liable under the plan may find it advisable to secure insurance coverage for part or all of their statutory liability. For this reason authorization for the purchase of such insurance is included in the act. The authorization is permissive rather than mandatory because experience under state and local tort liability has shown that in the case of large entities a self-insurance fund set aside by the governmental unit may be less expensive than insurance provided by an outside carrier. This decision is therefore left to the entity.

The liability provisions under the proposed Act have been tailored to provide relative certainty as to the amount of potential liability. Insurance carriers will not be faced with the possibility of astronomical awards which push premiums prohibitively skyward. Their experience with ordinary tort suits and with entity liability in some states has already provided sufficient information on the likely amounts of damage awards to set reasonable rates.

Likewise, the amounts of punitive damages are sufficiently well known to allow prediction (in the event that the entity is required to pay for punitive damages awarded against an officer). The only new provision for damages, that for constitutional-compensatory damages, is placed within definite statutory maxima and minima concerning liability—a factor which should allow easy computation of rates by the insurance carriers. Thus the lack of available insurance should not plague entities under the proposed statute.

The proposed legislation developed in this chapter has been designed to meet the remedial goals set forth at the outset of this study. Specific provision has been made for the payment of damages for the deprivation of the individual's constitutional rights per se regardless of the out-of-pocket expenses incurred by the plaintiff as a result of the deprivation. By setting a minimal amount in damages which must be awarded in any case in which the plaintiff prevails, the judgment of one cent—which cheapens the rights of all—has been rendered impossible. Further, the Act allows recovery for expenses incurred as the result of the constitutional deprivation. By thus combining what we have styled "constitutional-compensatory" and "compensatory" damages we have made provision for an adequate award in favor of the successful victim-plaintiff.

To avoid the pitfall of the noncollectable defendant which so often renders presently available remedies meaningless, the proposal insures recovery by making governmental entities directly responsible for a portion of the award and guarantor of the remaining amount. Combined with entity liability, however, is limited liability for individual officers for actions taken without proper regard for the constitutional rights of the individual in a manner consistent with the general principles of tort law and with the basic tenets of deterrence theory. While our primary aim is compensatory, the plan may have as an additional benefit an element of deterrence which will serve to decrease the incidence of constitutional deprivations committed by state officers.

By providing for the payment of costs incurred as a result of the constitutional deprivation, particularly the costs of defending against a criminal charge brought by an entity, and by providing for the clearing of the official record of the victim, the plan operates to remove official stigma and financial burden from the plaintiff who can prevail under the Act. The removal of the official records also has important extra-legal consequences for the victim-plaintiff in that he will not be haunted by an unconstitutionally developed record which might, for the rest of his days, discourage prospective employers, lead to difficulty in securing insurance, and otherwise impair the ordinary course of his daily activities.

The attorney's fee and costs provisions of the proposal are intended to operate in a fashion to provide the remedy even for those who are of most humble means. With the exception of the totally frivolous suit, invocation of the mechanisms devised will not result in financial hardships for the plaintiff even when he loses his case.

The venue provisions taken in conjunction with the placing of original jurisdiction in the general trial courts of the state reduce the possibility that a victim will be forced to bypass the remedy to which he is entitled because of the inconvenience of the forum in which the case must be tried.

Modification of the rules of evidence in civil actions has been undertaken to prevent the victim-plaintiff of "low status" from being denied relief solely because of his lack of status.

Finally, docket preference has been provided to avoid the potential quagmire of crowded courts which could postpone the plaintiff's recovery almost indefinitely. Particularly in the case of a plaintiff seeking declaratory relief against the enforcement of a legislative enactment, this provision is crucial, but it is also important in the overall sense that justice postponed is often justice denied.

It is submitted that the proposed legislative package meets the remedial requirements with which this study began. How adequately the plan will work in practice is of course an open question, but it at least possesses the potential to surpass the presently available remedies open to the victims of constitutional deprivations at the hands of state officers. Given the abysmal failure of the present mechanisms, even the potential of an adequate remedy is a great stride in the right direction. With this statute, or with one like it, we may at least begin to approach that "very essence of civil liberty" of which Chief Justice Marshall wrote. The goal is a noble one. It should not go unfulfilled for want of trying.

# Chapter 8

# Constitutional Remedies: A Look Forward

At the outset of this study, five standards were established by which to assess the adequacy of existing legal remedies for the violation of federal constitutional rights secured against invasion by state action. It was stated that an adequate remedy must provide compensation both for the constitutional deprivation per se and for any out-of-pocket expenses which are sustained as the result of deprivation; provide a source of recovery with sufficient assets to satisfy the judgment; remove, to the maximum extent feasible, the legal and extra-legal consequences of the deprivation; be readily available to all persons regardless of wealth or social status; and provide for speedy determination of the issues and satisfaction of judgment. Our thesis was that existing remedial devices provided by American law failed to meet these criteria.

In the examination of existing remedies four legal avenues were pursued. Two of these, suits against officers and suits against governmental entities, were originally created at least in part to provide compensation to the victims of legal injuries. The other two, the exclusionary rule and the criminal law, were not intended to provide a remedy in the sense that we have used the term but both were found to have at least limited remedial potential. Our examination, however, revealed serious shortcomings in these four legal devices. Neither individually nor in concert did they satisfy the standards against which they were measured. In some cases the reason was inherent in the device itself. In others a remedy that on its face appeared promising was found in practice not to fulfill the hope it offered. Thus it was concluded that present American law does not provide an adequate remedy for the victim of constitutional deprivations at the hands of state officers.

Having demonstrated the failure of present remedies and thereby having confirmed the thesis, an attempt was made to determine why orders of the Supreme Court—the authoritative interpreter of constitutional rights—did not command automatic obedience. It was suggested that we might profit from the application of concepts developed in the study of the capability of the President to command his subordinates in the executive branch of the national government. By utilizing the five factors of command set forth by Richard Neustadt, it was determined that the Supreme Court is not possessed of the capacity to issue self-executing orders for the protection of individual rights, and we concluded that the individual who would protect his rights must take up the sword himself.

The final portion of the study was devoted to developing a statute which could be utilized by the individual to secure redress for the violation of his federal constitutional rights. The proposal was specifically designed to meet the five criteria of adequacy by which the success or failure of presently available remedies was measured. On paper, at least, the statutory provisions advocated can lead to a vast improvement in the lot of the victim of unconstitutional state action. Because the proposed statute is just that—a proposed statute—its actual operation cannot yet be assessed, and for that reason there cannot really be a "conclusion" to this study.

The final test of the proposed legislation will not come in the pages of an academic exercise but in the arena of the real world in which individuals go about their task of living and are subjected, all too often, to constitutional deprivations by the same state governments whose very reason for existence is to serve the needs of those same individuals. The "final examination" for the statutory remedial scheme advocated in this inquiry will consist of questions such as the following: Are the benefits available to all elements of society; Is the remedy sure, and is it swift? If the proposal were to fail such examination, all of its "successes" as a theoretical remedy would be of no more value to the victim of a constitutional deprivation than is the success, such as it may be, of the present study in showing that current "remedies" are in reality abysmal failures in compensating that same victim. To him, the results would be identical.

What is offered here is the hope that the future will be an improvement over the past in terms of the remedies available to the victim of constitutional deprivations. Even if the proposed statute were to be adopted tomorrow, there would be no ironclad guarantee of success. Only time will tell whether the new remedy will prove more useful than the fruits of the Reconstruction Congresses which labored so mightily to produce so little. Only after the proposals of this study are put to the acid test of practical implementation in the real world will we know whether they truly guarantee that it will be possible for "every individual to claim the protection of the laws, whenever he receives an injury," and only then will it be possible to write a conclusion to this inquiry in the full sense of that term. Let us hope that when it is written it is not an epitaph.

# Appendix

# Model State Constitutional Deprivation Liability Act

## SECTION 1: DEFINITIONS

1.01—As used in this Act, "entity" shall mean the State or any of its subdivisions, including, but not limited to, counties, municipal corporations, districts, commissions, and boards.

1.02—As used in this Act, "officer" shall mean any person exercising the authority of any entity, whether or not employed by that entity.

1.03—As used in this Act "constitutional right" shall mean any right, privilege, or immunity secured against state action by the Constitution of the United States of America.

1.04—As used in this Act, "under color of law" shall mean under pretense of authority of an entity, whether or not authorized by law.

## SECTION 2: LIABILITY OF OFFICERS

2.01—Officers acting under color of law shall be subject to suit and liable for damages as provided in this Act for deprivations of constitutional rights.

2.02—Actions of officers resulting in deprivations of constitutional rights shall be divided into three classes: intentional, negligent, and due care.

2.03—An "intentional deprivation" is defined as an action taken with the specific intent to deprive an individual of his constitutional rights and resulting in said deprivation. An intentional deprivation shall result in officer liability of not less than one thousand dollars and not more than ten thousand dollars for each deprivation, provided however that nothing in this section shall preclude the assessment of punitive damages under the provisions of sections 5.04-5.05 of this Act.

2.04—A "negligent deprivation" is defined as an action taken without adherence to the standard of care which would have been exercised by a reasonable officer of like training and experience in the same or similar circumstances which results in a constitutional deprivation. A negligent deprivation shall result in officer liability of not less than one hundred dollars and not more than two hundred fifty dollars for each deprivation.

2.05—A "due care deprivation" is defined as a deprivation which is neither intentional nor negligent as defined in sections 2.03-2.04 of this Act. A due care deprivation shall not result in officer liability under this Act.

2.06—Good faith and reasonable reliance on a statute, ordinance, or other legislative or quasi-legislative enactment shall be considered as action undertaken with due care.

2.07—No legislative or quasi-legislative officer of any entity shall be held personally liable under the provisions of this Act for any action taken in the authorized course of his official legislative or quasi-legislative duties.

2.08—No judicial or quasi-judicial officer of any entity shall be held personally liable under the provisions of this Act for any action taken in the authorized course of the performance of his official judicial or quasi-judicial duties.

## SECTION 3: WAIVER OF IMMUNITY

3.01—The State of _____ and all of its subdivisions, hereinafter referred to collectively as "entities," shall be subject to suit and liable in damages, as provided in this Act, for violations of constitutional rights of individuals. The defense of immunity, both as to suit and as to liability, is hereby expressly waived and shall not be asserted by the entity or its insurer in any cause of action arising under this Act. No distinction shall be made between governmental and proprietary activities of any entity to defeat liability under this Act.

## SECTION 4: ENTITY LIABILITY

4.01—The entity shall be responsible for the satisfaction of the judgment, less the amount of officer liability, awarded for a constitutional violation committed by its officers acting under color of law.

4.02—The entity shall be responsible as guarantor of officer liability judgments. If the award against an officer-defendant shall not have been satisfied within ninety days from entry of final judgment, the plaintiff may notify the court of original jurisdiction of such fact under oath, and the court shall immediately upon receipt of such notification direct the entity to satisfy the amount of the judgment for which the officer is responsible within thirty days, provided however that if the entity shall have elected to satisfy the portion of the judgment for which it is directly responsible by payments at intervals under Sections 8.04–8.07 of this Act the amount still owing for officer liability shall be added to the remaining balance of entity liability. Failure to invoke this section within one year after the expiration of the ninety day period following entry of final judgment shall bar action by the plaintiff to require the entity to satisfy the officer-defendant's portion of the judgment.

4.03—No entity shall be held liable under the provisions of this Act for any deprivation of a constitutional right which shall occur as the result of the nondiscriminatory application of any statute, ordinance, rule, or other enactment duly passed by any legislative or quasi-legislative body unless the enactment shall first have been delcared to be in violation of the Constitution of the United States, either on its face or as applied, by a court of competent jurisdiction in a declaratory or other proceeding.

4.04—The trial courts of general jurisdiction of this State shall have jurisdiction to hear claims of unconstitutionality of statutes, ordinances, rules, or other enactments of any legislative or quasi-legislative body in this State in actions for declaratory judgments.

## SECTION 5: DAMAGES: TYPE AND AMOUNT

5.01—Damages under this Act shall be of three types: constitutional-compensatory, compensatory, and punitive.

5.02—Constitutional-compensatory damages shall be awarded for the deprivation of a constitutional right. A plaintiff prevailing in a cause of action arising under this Act shall be entitled to constitutional-compensatory damages of not less than one thousand dollars for each deprivation of a constitutional right as a matter of law. An award of constitutional-compensatory damages shall not exceed ten thousand dollars for any single deprivation.

5.03—Compensatory damages shall be awarded as in other civil actions, provided however that the amount shall not be less than the reasonable expenses incurred by the plaintiff as a result of the constitutional deprivation, including, but not limited to, medical expenses, investigatory costs in conjunction with the cause of action arising under this Act, and expenses incurred in the defense of any action, civil or criminal, commenced by an entity based wholly or in part on the fruits of a constitutional deprivation, provided however that such damages shall not be awarded for pain and suffering, mental anguish, or for attorney's fees in any cause of action arising under this Act. Nothing in this section shall be taken to exclude expenses not specifically enumerated herein from the class of expenses properly compensable under this Act in the absence of a specific exclusion.

5.04—Punitive damages shall be awarded in only two instances in causes of action arising under this Act:

(a) against entities, for enforcement of any statute, ordinance, or other enactment of any legislative or quasi-legislative body which previously has been declared unconstitutional, either on its face or as applied, as a matter of federal law by a court of competent jurisdiction; and

(b) against officers, for deprivations of constitutional rights resulting from intentional and willful action or from gross negligence and wanton disregard for the rights of the plaintiff.

5.05—Punitive damages shall be assessed in an amount consonant with the provisions of the law in other civil cases.

5.06—The methods and requirements for pleading damages shall be the same as in other civil cases.

### SECTION 6: INTEREST ON DAMAGES

6.01—Interest shall accrue on all compensatory and constitutional-compensatory damages under the provisions of this Act at a reasonable rate to be determined by the court and shall be assessed from the date of actual expenditure or loss until satisfaction of the judgment.

## SECTION 7: ADDITIONAL REMEDIES

7.01—If the victim of a constitutional deprivation actionable under the provisions of this Act shall have been made the subject of any official record or report which may reflect negatively upon said victim as a result of action initiated by any entity or officer based in whole or in part on the fruits of the constitutional deprivation, the court shall at the plaintiff's request order such report or record expunged.

7.02—In all proceedings subject to the laws of this state, whether public or private, the plaintiff who has successfully invoked Section 7.01 of this Act shall be entitled to deny that records ordered expunged have ever existed, and no entity or officer shall make known, or cause to be made known, any information to the contrary following the order of the court. No criminal or civil liability shall ever attach for the invocation of the provisions of this section.

7.03—Courts having jurisdiction to hear causes of action arising under this Act shall be authorized to fashion such additional remedies against entities and officers as shall be necessary to constitute a complete and adequate remedy.

## SECTION 8: SATISFACTION OF JUDGMENT

8.01—Unless an entity shall elect to satisfy a judgment entered under the provisions of this Act at intervals as provided in Sections 8.04-8.07 it shall pay in full that portion of the judgment for which it is directly responsible within thirty days from the entry of final judgment.

8.02—Payment shall be made by certified check to the plaintiff at his address of record, provided however that if such address is unknown said payment shall be made to the attorney of record for the plaintiff at said attorney's place of business.

8.03—Transmittal of the certified check required in section 8.02 shall be by registered mail.

8.04—Defendant entities in causes of action arising under this Act may elect to satisfy judgments for which they are responsible either directly or as guarantor by payments at intervals to be established with the approval of the court, provided however that the intervals shall not exceed one year between payments and that the total period of payment shall not exceed ten years from a date thirty days after the entry of final judgment.

8.05—Judgments satisfied by payments at intervals under Section 8.04 shall be subject to interest, payable to the plaintiff, at a reasonable rate to be determined by the court.

8.06—An entity may pay any portion or the total amount of the judgment in advance of the schedule established under Section 8.04.

8.07—The interest provided for in section 8.05 shall be in addition to any other interest found due under other provisions of this Act.

8.08—The provisions of Sections 8.04-8.07 shall be inapplicable to that portion of the judgment which shall be satisfied by an insurer of the entity.

## SECTION 9: ATTORNEY FEES

9.01—In all causes of action arising under this Act the prevailing plaintiff's counsel of record shall be entitled to an award of reasonable fees in an amount set by the court, which shall be taxed against the defendant entity and which shall in no instance be less than twenty-five percent of the amount awarded in damages, provided however that if counsel shall demonstrate to the satisfaction of the court that his customary fee in actions similar to those arising under this Act is greater than the minimum fee herein specified he shall be awarded the greater amount.

9.02—Attorney fees awarded under this section shall be in addition to the amount awarded in damages to the plaintiff.

9.03—In suits for declaratory judgments against an entity under the provisions of Section 4.04 counsel of record for the prevailing plaintiff shall be awarded reasonable fees by the court, provided that the fees awarded shall not be less than the amount customarily received by said counsel in declaratory judgment actions, or than the amount customary in the jurisdiction in which the action was tried in the event that the customary fees of counsel cannot be demonstrated to the satisfaction of the court.

9.04—Payment of attorney fees awarded under this Act shall be made directly to the attorney of record for the plaintiff within thirty days of the entry of final judgment, unless the entity shall elect to satisfy the judgment by payments at intervals as provided in Sections 8.04-8.07 of this Act, in which case the attorney fees shall be paid in a like manner and with like interest.

9.05—No attorney shall request or receive, from the plaintiff in any cause of action arising under this Act or from any other source, any fee or other compensation for his services not provided for in Sections 9.01-9.04. Violation of this section shall be a misdemeanor punishable by forfeiture of both the properly awarded attorney's fees and the amounts collected in violation of this section. In addition, any person found guilty of violating this section shall be fined not less than five hundred dollars nor more than one thousand dollars for each offense and may be imprisoned for a term not to exceed one year for each offense.

9.06—Fees forfeited under Section 9.05 shall be returned to the treasurer or other appropriate officer of the entity against which they were taxed, and amounts received in violation of Section 9.05 shall be returned to the party who shall have paid them, provided that if the identity of said party cannot be determined the amount forfeited shall likewise be paid over to the treasurer or other appropriate officer of the entity against which attorney's fees were taxed. All sums collected as fines shall be disposed of as otherwise provided by the laws of this state.

## SECTION 10: COURT COSTS

10.01—In causes of action arising under this Act costs shall not be assessed against the plaintiff, provided however that this section shall be inapplicable if the court shall find that the claim asserted by the plaintiff is frivolous and totally without legal merit.

## SECTION 11: JURISDICTION AND VENUE; CHANGE OF VENUE

11.01—Original jurisdiction in causes of action arising under this Act shall be in the trial courts of general jurisdiction of this state. Appellate jurisdiction shall be the same as provided by statute for other civil actions.

11.02—Venue shall be in the court of general jurisdiction for the county in which the plaintiff resides, in which the deprivation is alleged to have occurred, or in which the entity shall have its principal office, at the election of the plaintiff.

11.03—Changes of venue shall be taken as in other civil actions.

11.04—In those courts which shall sit in divisions, the presiding judge may designate one or more divisions to hear all causes of action arising under this Act, subject to the provisions of Section 14.

## SECTION 12: PROCEDURE AND EVIDENCE

12.01—Unless otherwise provided in this Act, the rules of procedure and evidence generally applicable in civil proceedings shall apply in causes of action arising under this Act.

12.02—Evidence or testimony concerning criminal charges or proceedings against the plaintiff in a cause of action arising under this Act which have been determined by a court of competent jurisdiction to have been based in whole or in part upon the fruits of a constitutional deprivation alleged by the plaintiff in a cause of action arising under this Act shall be inadmissible in said cause of action, provided however that the resolution of the constitutional claims in favor of the defendant in said criminal action shall be admissible at the discretion of the plaintiff in proceedings under this Act.

12.03—Statements made in the presence of the court or jury, or actions taken in the presence of the court or jury, which shall have the effect of making known information which would be precluded by Section 12.02 shall be grounds for a mistrial at the option of the plaintiff.

12.04—Willful violation of Sections 12.02-12.03 shall be a misdemeanor punishable by a fine not to exceed five hundred dollars, and shall further result in civil liability in the same manner as a constitutional deprivation under this Act, provided that said civil liability shall not be less than two hundred fifty nor more than five hundred dollars.

## SECTION 13: TRIAL BY JURY

13.01—Trial by jury is preserved in causes of action arising under this Act, provided however that a jury may be waived by consent of all parties to the action.

## SECTION 14: DOCKET PREFERENCE

14.01—Causes of action arising under this Act shall be given docket preference over all other civil actions with the exception of challenges to election returns.

14.02—Suits for declaratory relief under this Act shall have docket preference over suits for money damages under this Act.

14.03—In those jurisdictions in which the presiding judge has designated one or more judges or divisions of the court to hear all causes of action arising under this Act, pursuant to the provisions of Section 11.04, the docket preference herein provided shall be inapplicable in other divisions, or in cases before other judges, provided however that if a cause shall not have been heard within one hundred eighty days after its filing the presiding judge shall transfer said cause of action to another division or judge on motion of any party and the docket preference provided in Sections 14.01-14.02 shall apply.

### SECTION 15: EXCLUSIVITY OF REMEDY

15.01—Institution of an action under the provisions of this Act shall bar any other civil remedy sought by the same plaintiff against the same defendant-entity or -officer for damages arising out of the same act or occurrence. Institution of an action in the courts of this State or of the United States for damages arising out of an act or occurrence which would otherwise give rise to a cause of action under this Act shall bar any suit or recovery under this Act.

### SECTION 16: INFORMAL SETTLEMENT

16.01—Nothing in this Act shall operate to bar informal settlement of claims arising hereunder in a manner consistent with the provisions of Sections 16.01-16.03.

16.02—No settlement shall be for an amount less than the minimum amount established by law for the constitutional-compensatory damages claimed plus the actual out-of-pocket expenses alleged.

16.03—No settlement shall be made without the approval of the court having jurisdiction over the cause of action.

### SECTION 17: INSURANCE

17.01—Entities are hereby authorized to purchase insurance for part or all of their liability for constitutional deprivations.

# Notes

## CHAPTER 1: CONSTITUTIONAL REMEDIES

1.  Marbury v. Madison, 5 U.S. (1 Cranch) 137, 165 (1803). Cases will be cited by name and date in the text. A full citation to the United States Report appears in the Table of Cases, and a footnote page citation appears in the case of material quoted at length from an opinion. Supreme Court Reporter citations are employed for decisions for which United States Reports citations were not available at the time of preparation. Citations to the lower federal courts will indicate jurisdiction and date in the text, with full citations in the Table of Cases.

2.  Wright, "The Law of Remedies as a Social Institution," 18 U. Detroit L.J. 376 (1955). Wright suggests the categories of compensation, specific relief, restitution, punishment, and prevention in his functional analysis of legal remedies.

3.  Article VI, Paragraph 2, provides: "This Constitution, and the Laws of the United States which shall be made in Pursuance thereof; and all Treaties made, or which shall be made, under the Authority of the United States, shall be the Supreme Law of the Land; and the Judges in every State shall be bound thereby, any Thing in the Constitution or Laws of any State to the Contrary notwithstanding."

4.  Dworkin, "Taking Rights Seriously," N.Y. Review of Books, December 17, 1970, at 23.

5.  Gellhorn and Lauer, "Federal Liability for Personal and Property Damage," 29 N.Y.U.L. Rev. 1325 (1954). See also, Note, "Private Bills in Congress," 79 Harv. L. Rev. 1684 (1966).

6.  Marbury v. Madison (1803). See also Hamilton's preliminary groundwork in Federalist No. 78.

7.  Chisholm v. Georgia (1793) is discussed at length in Chapter 3.

8.  Plessy v. Ferguson (1896) established the now discredited doctrine of "separate but equal" facilities for individuals of different races, and Hammer v. Dagenhart (1918) temporarily limited the power of Congress to control child labor through the commerce power.

9.  See particularly, Wasby, *The Impact of the United States Supreme Court* (1970), and Becker and Feeley, *The Impact of Supreme Court Decisions* (2d ed. 1973).

10.  Mention might also be made of the relationship between the federal district courts and state authorities which arises from the federal habeas corpus power. This

does not alter the Supreme Court's superior position, but it does provide another route by which to reach it by "starting over again" at the bottom of the inferior judicial pyramid. This possibility is indicated by the contact of the two lower pyramids at their bases, but given the Supreme Court's current attitude in favor of decreasing habeas proceedings it is not stressed in the text. See Stone v. Powell, 96 S.Ct. 3037 (1976).

Of course, to be perfectly accurate, in this diagram there would have to be eleven federal inferior judicial pyramids (one for each of the circuits) and 50 state judicial pyramids (some with an intermediate appellate layer). The clarity gained by the simplification seems well worth the accuracy sacrificed.

## CHAPTER 2: SUITS AGAINST THE OFFICER

1.　At the time of the Monroe decision they were only allegations, because the trial court had dismissed the complaint and the Court of Appeals had affirmed the dismissal. Thus the case came before the Supreme Court on the pleadings alone, without benefit of a finding of fact by the lower courts. While for the purposes of the appeal the allegations were taken as true they remained no more than the plaintiff's assertions until the trial court heard and decided the case on remand.

2.　An important issue was also raised concerning the liability of the employing entity, but that point will be reserved for the consideration of entity liability as a separate topic.

3.　These cases are treated in full in Chapter 5, which deals with the federal criminal law and constitutional deprivations brought about by state officials.

4.　Monroe v. Pape, 365 U.S. 167, 192 (1961) Harlan and Stewart, JJ., concurring).

5.　Ibid. at 183.

6.　Even so, the section has not become a complete catchall. See Paul v. Davis, 96 S.Ct. 1155 (1976), holding that defamation by a state official is not a constitutional-rights violation (and hence not actionable under Section 1983) even though it may give rise to a state tort law action.

7.　Tenney v. Brandhove, 341 U.S. 367, 376 (1951).

8.　Pierson v. Ray, 386 U.S. 547, 553, 554 (1967).

9.　Even Justice Douglas showed some sympathy for his brethren of the robe. At page 556, he supports immunity for honest errors.

10.　Imbler v. Pachtman, 96 S.Ct. 984, 993 (1976).

11.　Pierson v. Ray, 386 U.S. 547, 557 (1967).

12.　Scheuer v. Rhodes, 416 U.S. 232, 247, 248 (1974).

13.　Wood v. Strickland, 95 S.Ct. 992, 1001 (1975).

14.　Unfortunately, statistical data are not available from the Administrative Office of the United States Courts to provide the basis of an analysis similar to that conducted in Chapter 5 of a ten-year pattern of prosecutions under 18 U.S.C. Section 242, the criminal statute dealing with state officer deprivations of federal rights accomplished under color of law.

15.　Knuckles v. Prasse, 435 F.2d 1255 (3d Cir. 1970).

16.　Cordova v. Chonko, 315 F. Supp. 953, 964 (N.D. Ohio 1970). It should be noted, in fairness to the trial judge, that the court ordered the lad reinstated in school under the equitable remedy provision of Section 1983. Another case of similar characteristics is Magnett v. Pelletier, 488 F.2d 33 (1st Cir. 1973), in which the Court of Appeals reduced a constitutional-rights-deprivation judgment of $500 to the amount of one dollar on the grounds that the trial court had used the word "nominal" in setting the $500 amount. While admitting that the award of damages for constitutional-rights deprivations as such is permitted under Section 1983, the First Circuit seems to have undermined the spirit of the law by its insistence on a strict dictionary meaning of the word "nominal" instead of concentrating on the deprivation of constitutional rights.

17.   Whirl v. Kern, 407 F.2d 781, 798 (5th Cir. 1969). The victim had been held in jail some nine months, because of apparently negligent paperwork, after all charges against him had been dismissed.
18.   Gaston v. Gibson, 328 F. Supp. 3, 4 (E.D. Tenn. 1969). For additional examples of punitive damages, see Aldridge v. Mullins, 377 F. Supp. 850 (M.D. Tenn. 1972); Lykken v. Vavreck, 366 F. Supp. 585 (D. Minn. 1973); Davidson v. Dixon, 386 F. Supp. 482 (D. Del. 1974), affd. 529 F.2d 511 (3d Cir. 1975); Lamb v. Cartwright, 393 F. Supp. 1081 (E.D. Tex. 1975), affd. 524 F.2d 238 (5th Cir. 1975).
19.   Davidson v. Dixon, 529 F.2d 511 (3d Cir. 1975).
20.   Those officers who happen to have accumulated some measure of wealth, presumably from some source outside their employment, have been known to render themselves judgment-proof by conveying their assets to their wives. This makes tort recovery impossible, but woe unto the officer whose wife is not of the faithful variety. A divorce decree could well place him in the other, less desirable, judgment-proof category in short order.
21.   In addition to 42 U.S.C. Section 1983, see 42 U.S.C. Sections 1341, 1343(3), which confer federal jurisdiction without regard for diversity of citizenship or amount in controversy in civil rights cases.
22.   This jurisdictional springboard effect is not without some value. It has been asserted that the federal forum provides the benefits of escaping from strict common law legal requirements, providing a forum free from local or municipal administrative pressures, and an increasing measure of damages. See Note, "Civil Rights Act Section 1983: Abuses by Law Enforcement Officers," 36 Indiana L.J. 317, 321 (1961).
23.   For those interested in the vagaries of official tort liability in general, an excellent summary is available in Kenneth Culp Davis' *Administrative Law Treatise* (1958) and supplemental volumes (1970 and 1976).
24.   Foote, "Tort Remedies for Police Violation of Individual Rights," 39 Minn. L. Rev. 493 (1955).
25.   Ibid. at 498.
26.   Recognition of the failure of the common law remedies in the area of search and seizure violations is one of the factors which motivated the Supreme Court to extend the "exclusionary rule" to state criminal trials. A discussion of the exclusionary rule is found in Chapter 4.
27.   The judgment-proof-defendant phenomenon presents what might be called a reverse-poverty effect. The likelihood of initiation of proceedings depends on a standard of wealth, with the most fortunate in terms of wealth being the least fortunate in terms of attractiveness as a potential defendant in a tort action.
28.   Foote, op. cit. at 500.
29.   On the civil death problem, see Foote, op. cit. at 507 ff.
30.   Even the illusion has worried some commentators. See Mathes and Jones, "Toward a 'Scope of Official Duty' Immunity for Police Officers in Damage Actions," 53 Georgetown L.J. 889 (1963).

## CHAPTER 3: SUITS AGAINST THE GOVERNMENT

1.   Actually, the British subject may well have been in a more favorable position. A major legal loophole, the "petition of right," was developed to allow recovery in many instances. This remedy is discussed briefly later in the chapter.
2.   Borchard, "Government Responsibility in Tort," 36 Yale L.J. 1 (1926).
3.   Watkins, *The State as a Party Litigant* 1-4 (1927).
4.   Prosser, *Torts* 996 (3d ed. 1964).
5.   *Black's Law Dictionary* 1130 (Rev. 4th ed. 1968).
6.   1 Blackstone, *Commentaries on the Laws of England* 185 (1856 ed.).
7.   Borchard, op. cit. at 21 ff; Spiegel, *The Illinois Court of Claims* 4 (1962).
8.   Presumably Henry VIII laid this potential "remedy" to rest once and for all in the English common law.

9.    Spiegel, *The Illinois Court of Claims* (1962), 5, 6, and sources there cited; contra, Borchard, op. cit. at 23.

10.    Borchard, op. cit. at 32; Spiegel, op. cit. at 5; Watkins, op. cit. at 7; Fratcher, "Sovereign Immunity in Probate Proceedings," 31 Mo. L. Rev. 127, 128 (1966); Mikva, "Sovereign Immunity: In a Democracy the Emperor Has No Clothes," 1966 U. Ill. L.F. 828, 846; Lawyer, "Birth and Death of Governmental Immunity," 15 Clev.-Mar. L. Rev. 529 (1966).

11.    Blackstone, op. cit. at 182.

12.    Ibid.

13.    Borchard, op. cit, at 31; Watkins, op. cit. at 11; Spiegel, op. cit. at 6; Prosser, op. cit. at 997.

14.    "Government" is used here in its broad sense rather than in the more limited meaning of the prime minister and his cabinet, in the British manner.

15.    On the petition of right generally, see Watkins, op. cit. at 14–31.

16.    Fratcher, op. cit. at 129.

17.    Watkins, op. cit. at 23, citing Tobin v. Regina, 33 L.J.P.C. 199, 16 C.B.N.S. 310, 10 L.T. 762 (1864).

18.    Fratcher, op. cit. at 128 ff.

19.    Mathis, "The Eleventh Amendment: Adoption and Interpretation," 2 Georgia L. Rev. 207 (1968).

20.    The quotations which follow are taken from page 673 of the opinions.

21.    See Hargrove v. Town of Cocoa Beach, 90 So. 2d 130 (Fla. 1957), discussed below.

22.    Main, *The Anti-Federalists* 157 (1964 ed.).

23.    Ibid. at 155; Spiegel, op. cit. at 15, 16.

24.    *The Federalist Papers* 487, 488 (Rossiter ed. 1961).

25.    Main, op. cit. at 157.

26.    Mathis, op. cit. at 214–217.

27.    See the dissent of Justice Iredell in Chisholm v. Georgia, 2 U.S. (2 Dall.) 419, 434, 435 (1793).

28.    Ibid. at 449, 450.

29.    Opinion of Justice Cushing in Chisholm at 468.

30.    Mathis, op. cit. at 223.

31.    Ibid. at 224, 225, 229.

32.    The Senate vote was 23–2, and the House approved 89–1. Mathis, op. cit. at 227.

33.    See Pugh, "Historical Approach to the Doctrine of Sovereign Immunity," 13 Louisiana L. Rev. 476, 485 (1953).

34.    The categories here are taken in large part from Mathis, op. cit., and the cases there cited.

35.    City of Kenosha, Wisconsin v. Bruno, 412 U.S. 507, 513 (1973).

36.    Borchard, "Government Liability in Tort," 34 Yale L.J. 1, 4, 5 (1924).

37.    Mikva, op. cit. at 846.

38.    See, Leflar and Kantrowitz, "Tort Liability of the States," 29 N.Y.U.L. Rev. 1363 (1954); Cooperrider, "The Court, the Legislature, and Governmental Tort Liability," 72 Mich. L. Rev. 187 (1973).

39.    Prosser, op. cit. at 1001.

40.    The passage is quoted in Kramer, "The Governmental Tort Immunity Doctrine in the United States 1790–1955," 1966 U. Ill. L.F. 795, 804.

41.    The Bailey case is singled out as the first of its type in Kramer, op. cit. at 816.

42.    California Law Revision Commission, *A Study Relating to Sovereign Immunity* 222 (1963).

43.    For a summary of the criticism voiced before World War II see Repko, "American Legal Commentary on the Doctrines of Municipal Tort Liability," 9 Law & Contemp. Prob. 214 (1942).

44.    This lineage is suspect, as indicated above in the discussion of the separate

origins of sovereign and local immunity. The Florida court goes on to mention Devon, but proceeds to discount it because it was decided after the Declaration of Independence, although this approach has also been questioned, above, in light of the precedent cited by the Justices in the Devon case which long antedated even the founding of the Jamestown settlement on American soil.

45. The Florida court was unwilling to go to all logical extremes. Dicta in the Hargrove opinion clearly indicated that the court was unwilling to include judicial, quasi-judicial, legislative, or quasi-legislative activities in the category which, by application of the doctrine of respondeat superior, would bring about municipal tort liability.

46. Davis, *Administrative Law of the Seventies* 551 (1976). Thirty-four states had some form of waiver statute. Ibid. at 555.

47. Molitor v. Kaneland Community Unit District No. 302, 163 N.E.2d 89 (Ill. 1959).

48. Stone v. Arizona Highway Commission, 381 P.2d 107 (Ariz. 1963).

49. Parish v. Pitts, 429 S.W. 2d 45 (Ark. 1968).

50. Muskopf v. Corning Hospital District, 359 P.2d 457 (Cal. 1961).

51. For examples of legislatures restoring immunity, see Davis, op. cit. at 556.

52. According to Davis, 43 states now have some form of liability. Ibid. at 557.

## CHAPTER 4: THE EXCLUSIONARY RULE

1. See Miranda v. Arizona, 384 U.S. 436 (1966), and its progeny.

2. For a thorough history of the rule's development, see Allen, "Federalism and the Fourth Amendment," 1961 Supreme Court Review 1.

3. Olmstead v. United States, 277 U.S. 438, 477 (1928).

4. Ibid. at 470.

5. Ibid. at 485.

6. See Oaks, "Studying the Exclusionary Rule in Search and Seizure," 37 U. Chicago L. Rev. 665, 670 (1970).

7. See Oaks, op. cit.; LaFave and Remington, "Controlling the Police: The Judge's Role in Making and Revising Law Enforcement Decisions," 63 Mich. L. Rev. 987 (1965); and Allen, op. cit.

8. This assumes the absence of malicious prosecution of a defendant known by the prosecuting authorities to be innocent. The possibility of such prosecution is recognized, but the instance of such proceedings is excluded from consideration in this study.

9. LaFave, "Improving Police Performance through the Exclusionary Rule—Part I: Current Police and Local Court Practices," 30 Mo. L. Rev. 391, 398–403 (1965).

10. Wigmore, "Using Evidence Obtained by Illegal Search and Seizure," 8 A.B.A.J. 479, 482 (1922).

11. Lest the reader believe that the author has lost control of his imagination, atttention is directed to the case of Miller V. United States discussed at length in Chapter 5.

12. A coerced confession situation would be essentially the same as the planted evidence case insofar as the operation of the rule to the benefit of the innocent individual is concerned.

13. The term "factual guilt" is used to distinguish the breaking of a law in fact from "legal guilt" in which the breach has been proven in a court of law according to proper legal procedures. See Packer, "Two Models of the Criminal Process," 113 U. Pa. L. Rev. 1 (1964).

14. The failure of the rule as a remedy should not bring criticism on its creators. As was noted earlier its purpose is said to be to prevent, not to remedy.

15. Oaks, op. cit.

16. Ibid.

17. It is difficult to understand how exclusion and the result of acquittal can be

sufficient sanction for the "threat" in direct deterrence while it is insufficient in the special deterrence sense. In neither situation would there appear to be direct punishment of the offending officer. Oaks does not attempt to explain this point, but the difference—while important in theory—need not detain us here. For our purposes, as should become clear, it makes little difference whether we call the deterrent effect of the rule "special" or "direct." Both are concerned with the officer's weighing future conduct in cost-benefit fashion.

18. Oaks, op. cit. at 711, 712. The three aspects of indirect deterrence in the text are taken from the Oaks discussion.

19. LaFave, *Arrest: The Decision to Take a Suspect into Custody* (1965).

20. Skolnick, *Justice without Trial: Law Enforcement in a Democratic Society* (1966).

21. See, for example, Wald, Ayres, Hess, Schantz, and Whitebread, "Interrogations in New Haven: The Impact of Miranda," 76 Yale L.J. 1521 (1967); Medalie, Zeitz, and Alexander, "Custodial Police Interrogation in Our Nation's Capital: The Attempt to Implement Miranda," 66 Mich. L. Rev. 1347 (1968).

22. The terminology is Skolnick's. More detailed consideration of this view of the appellate courts will be forthcoming in Chapter 6 in conjunction with the perceived legitimacy of the Supreme Court as a constitutional command-giver.

23. This appears to be the only present cost, given Oaks' finding of the absence of internal police discipline and the evidence on the lack of criminal prosecutions (see Chapter 5).

24. One might question whether there is not a significant difference between the "special" and "direct" aspects from a communications perspective.

25. People v. Cahan, 282 P.2d 905, 913 (Cal. 1955).

26. Katz v. United States, 289 U.S. 347 (1967).

27. As noted above, the rule is of value only in a trial setting. If there is no trial even this means of detection is lost, and the violation may go undetected altogether.

28. Burns, "Mapp v. Ohio: An All American Mistake," 19 DePaul L. Rev. 80, 95 (1969).

29. Oaks, op. cit. at 739, 740.

30. Skolnick, op. cit. at 215.

31. For an analysis suggesting that just such activities took place in Chicago, see Dash, "Cracks in the Foundation of Criminal Justice," 46 Ill. L. Rev. 385, 390–392 (1951).

32. LaFave, *Arrest* (1965). The states included were Kansas, Michigan, and Wisconsin.

33. Allen, op. cit. at 39.

34. LaFave, op. cit. at 473.

35. LaFave, "Improving Police Performance through the Exclusionary Rule—Part I: Current Police and Local Court Practices," 30 Mo. L. Rev. 391, 445 (1965).

36. Oaks, op. cit. at 681.

37. Remember that Oaks had already ruled out special deterrence.

38. See Oaks, op. cit. at 731; Skolnick, op. cit. at 224, 225; LaFave, op. cit. at 421, 422.

39. Oaks, op. cit. at 731.

40. For a wide-ranging critique of the Harris decision, see Dershowitz and Ely, "Harris v. New York, Some Anxious Observations on the Candor and Logic of the Emerging Nixon Majority," 80 Yale L.J. 1198 (1971). For a careful attack on the majority position in Calandra, see Schrock and Welsh, "Up from Calandra: The Exclusionary Rule as a Constitutional Requirement," 59 Minn. L. Rev. 251 (1974).

41. For an early, and rather optimistic, study on this point, see Nagel, "Testing the Effects of Excluding Illegally Seized Evidence," 1965 Wisc. L. Rev. 283. Later, more critical, evaluations of police training methods have already been noted.

## CHAPTER 5: FEDERAL CRIMINAL LAW

1.   The major part of the remainder of this chapter appeared in its original form as Spurrier, "McAlester and After: Section 242, Title 18 of the United States Code and the Protection of Civil Rights," 11 Tulsa L.J. 347 (1976). The author expresses his appreciation to the editors of the *Tulsa Law Journal* for permission to use the material here.

2.   The only mention of the section came in passing references in Bowman v. Chicago & Northwestern Ry. Co. (1885), a private civil suit; Hodges v. United States (1906), a criminal conspiracy action against a private party defendant; and O'Sullivan v. Felix (1914), another private civil proceeding.

3.   Screws v. United States, 325 U.S. 91, 139 (1944) (Roberts, Frankfurter and Jackson, J.J. dissenting). Prior to the creation of the Civil Rights Section in the Department of Justice there were only four reported cases involving prosecutions under Section 242. See Caldwell and Brodie, "Enforcement of the Criminal Civil Rights Statute, 18 U.S.C. Section 242, in Prison Brutality Cases," 52 Geo. L.J. 706, 707 (1964).

4.   Although the primary election aspect of the case is not of crucial importance to the development of Section 242, this holding presaged Smith v. Allwright (1944), which struck down the white primary as violative of the Constitution.

5.   United States v. Classic, 313 U.S. 299, 326 (1941).

6.   Ibid. at 341.

7.   One other issue of construction in Classic involved the defense contention that there could be no violation unless differential penalties were inflicted upon the victim because of his race, etc. The Court rejected this view, holding that the section created two separate crimes—deprivation of rights secured or protected on the one hand and infliction of differing penalties on the other.

8.   The maximum penalty under the section at the time of the Screws case was one-year imprisonment and a fine of $1,000. The life imprisonment penalty for deprivations resulting in death was not added until 1968.

9.   Screws v. United States (1944) at 111.

10.   The United States Reports do not indicate the author of the opinion.

11.   Screws v. United States (1944) at 139. For a contrary view see Alfange, "Under Color of Law," 47 Cornell L.Q. 395 (1962).

12.   On remand the case was again tried before a jury, and all defendants were acquitted. They subsequently returned to their duties as law enforcement officers. See Shapiro, "Limitations in Prosecuting Civil Rights Violations," 46 Cornell L.Q. 532, 535 (1961). The Screws specific intent rule is often blamed for the failure to secure a Section 242 conviction. Shapiro reports the comments of a jury foreman who indicated that although there was a consensus that the defendant was guilty of manslaughter or second degree murder and that the state should do something about it in a criminal action, the jury felt bound by the judge's instructions under the Screws rule to acquit the defendant of the misdemeanor charged under Section 242.

13.   Pritchett, *The Roosevelt Court* 152 (1948).

14.   Williams v. United States, 341 U.S. 97, 101 (1951) (citations omitted).

15.   United States v. Price, 383 U.S. 787, 794, 795 (1966).

16.   18 U.S.C. Section 241 is the conspiracy section of the civil rights statutes.

17.   United States v. Price, 383 U.S. 787, 806 (1966).

18.   The dates are based on fiscal years. The data collection periods used by the Administrative Office of the United States Courts are fiscal years, and there is no convenient method for translating the data into calendar years.

19.   Section 241 involves conspiracy to deprive of rights; Section 242, acts under color of law; Section 243, racially motivated exclusion from juries; Section 244, public accommodations discrimination against persons wearing the uniform of the United States armed forces.

20. Director of the Administrative Office of the United States Courts, *Annual Report* 250 (1976).
21. Ibid.
22. Oaks, "Studying the Exclusionary Rule in Search and Seizure," 37 U. Chicago L. Rev. 665 (1970). Data are developed from his Table 5.
23. Both the deputies and their victims were white, so this is not a case of racially motivated abuse.
24. Miller v. United States, 404 F.2d 611, 612 (5th Cir. 1968).
25. Shapiro, op. cit., at 545–546.
26. In the Miller case, above, a witness for the prosecution was a fellow deputy sheriff of the defendants. This factor, no doubt, facilitated the conviction. In the eyes of the jury, the credibility of the victims' testimony was no doubt enhanced.
27. See Note, "Discretion to Prosecute Federal Civil Rights Crimes," 74 Yale L.J. 1297 (1965).
28. Caldwell and Brodie, op. cit. at 740.
29. The "good" effect here is more a postulate than a demonstrated fact presented by these writers. Of course, so is the potential "bad" effect of the object lesson noted in rebuttal, but until the impact of acquittals on perceptions and behavior of state officials who might otherwise undertake unconstitutional activities is examined in a thorough study, it would seem that either "educative effect" is possible. Certainly one cannot rule out the "bad" and accept the "good" effect by mere fiat.
30. At least one writer minces no words about trial by ordeal. See Yale L.J. note cited in note 27, above, where it is argued, "Even an acquittal would serve as a deterrent and restraining function by exposing a criminal defendant to the ordeal of trial. If this constitutes harassment of a defendant ultimately acquitted, it is not illegal harassment, so long as the Justice Department has cause to believe him guilty. And if the ordeal of trial serves in any way to deter unlawful actions, it is not only legal but desirable."
31. A more detailed discussion of the aspects of deterrence appears in the context of the exclusionary rule in Chapter 4.
32. The discussion in this chapter has centered on the federal criminal law that has developed around 18 U.S.C. Section 242. In a federal system such as ours there is also the possibility of the state prosecuting its own officers for civil rights violations, but the practice has been not to do so.

## CHAPTER 6: REMEDIES AND REALITIES

1. Neustadt, *Presidential Power* (1961).
2. While praising Neustadt's work as "one of the few truly significant statements about the American presidency," Peter Sperlich has taken him to task for relying almost entirely upon the formal aspects of power. See Sperlich, "Bargaining and Overload: An Essay on Presidential Power," in Wildavsky, *Perspectives on the Presidency* 406 (1975). Sperlich suggests that the model is "not accurate in its almost complete disregard of unilateral controls other than command of non-instrumental influence relationships." Particularly, he is concerned with "interpersonal identification" which would lead a president to select subordinates on the basis of personal loyalty, for example, and "non-command unilateral action" which he feels is more likely to occur in situations less dramatic than those examined by Neustadt.

What is most important for our purposes is not the validity, real or potential, of the criticisms but rather the fact that insofar as we are concerned with the Supreme Court and state officers they are nearly totally inapplicable. Neither the Court as a whole nor individual justices are likely to be able to select "subordinates" on the basis of personal loyalty. Even if a particular justice may from time to time have the President's ear on federal judicial appointments, many other factors will also be involved in the nomination and confirmation process, and of course while justices serve indefinite terms the Presidents will come and go at fairly regular intervals. No matter how influential a particular justice might be with one chief executive, it is unlikely that his influence will carry over to a line of successors. Beyond this, however, lies the reality that even this limited influence is unlikely to extend to the state judiciary(most especially in those states in which judges are chosen by popular election), and it is well nigh impossible that a justice will be able to exert influence over the staffing of the multitude of executive positions which exist in the fifty states.

As for the "non-command unilateral action" category, Sperlich suggests that many presidential requests are acted upon without bargaining and without command, particularly in routine matters. This may well be true, but on the Supreme Court side "requests" are seldom found when constitutional rights are at stake, and the very fact that the Court hears and decides a case indicates that at least four justices feel that it is something more than "routine." We are left, then, with Neustadt's five factors as our point of departure.

3.    Davis, *The National Executive Branch* 103 (1970).

4.    Davis' work is concerned primarily with the workings of the national bureaucracy, but its more general organizational approach has obvious relevance for a broader context.

5.    This statement assumes that the Court is not evenly divided on the constitutional issue. It is also assumed that the Court has issued a ruling on the merits of the constitutional issue rather than deciding the case on narrower grounds or disposing of it by such procedural means as dismissing its own writ of certiorari as having been improvidently granted.

6.    Spurrier and Schaub, Missouri Fire Safety Inspections–A Study of Compliance, June, 1968 (unpublished paper).

7.    Camara v. Municipal Court (1967) and See v. Seattle (1967).

8.    For a discussion of the problem of communications in the context of the exclusionary rule, see Chapter 4.

9.    Lest we hastily relegate this phenomenon to the shelf of historical curiosity, it should be noted that in recent "landmark" cases the performance of the Burger Court has been highly reminiscent of the work of John Jay and his colleagues. See, for example, New York Times Co. v. United States (1971), the "Pentagon Papers" case, and Furman v. Georgia (1972), the death penalty case, in which all nine members of the Court felt compelled to give individual expression to their views.

10.    Even Marshall could be confusing at times. See Gibbons v. Ogden (1824), where he seems to give Congress almost unlimited commerce power only to withdraw it in part.

11.    Murphy and Tanenhaus, *The Study of Public Law* 158 (1972).

12.    Burns, "Mapp v. Ohio: An All American Mistake," 19 DePaul L. Rev. 80, 100 (1969).

13.    Howard, "On the Fluidity of Judicial Choice," 62 Am. Pol. Sci. Rev. 43 (1968). See also, Murphy, *Elements of Judicial Strategy* (1964).

14.    Bivens v. Six Unknown Named Agents of Federal Bureau of Narcotics (1971) (Harlan, J., concurring).

15.    Sometimes the issue facing the Court may be one which defies precise solution. The formula of "all deliberate speed" in school desegregation was no model of clarity, to be sure, but given the multitude of local fact situations which would face the federal district courts after the Brown decision flexibility was essential to reasonable implementation. The admitted fact that some lower courts were less than zealous in their pursuit of the Brown goals should not blind us to the fact that in this first bold step in the desegregation of public primary and secondary schools the Supreme Court had very little in the way of a road map.

16.    Miranda v. Arizona (1966).

17.    The situation in which the officer fails to respond because of competing pressures to "get his man" is discussed later under the heading of legitimacy of the command giver.

18. Wilson, *Varieties of Police Behavior* (1968); Skolnick, *Justice without Trial* (1966).
19. Wasby, *The Impact of the United States Supreme Court: Some Perspectives* (1970).
20. Packer, "Two Models of the Criminal Process," 113 U. Pa. L. Rev. 1 (1964). Essentially the same material is also included as chapter 8 of Packer, *The Limits of the Criminal Sanction* (1968).
21. See Wasby, op. cit.
22. "To be just to these people means to give each what he deserves by how he acts and talks. This is close to the ancient conception of 'distributive' justice, which holds that things and honors should be divided among persons according to merit or so that inequality in person is reflected by a proportional inequality in treatment." Wilson, op. cit. at 36.
23. Ibid. at 37.
24. Skolnick, op. cit. at 228.

CHAPTER 7: TOWARD A MORE ADEQUATE REMEDY

1. See, for example, Littlefield, "Stare Decisis, Prospective Overruling, and Judicial Legislation in the Context of Sovereign Immunity," 9 St. L.U.L. Rev. 56 (1964); Peck, "The Role of Courts and Legislatures in the Reform of Tort Law," 48 Minn. L. Rev. 265 (1963); Note, "Tort Liability of the State: A Proposal for Maine," 16 Maine L. Rev. 209 (1964); Note, "The Role of the Courts in Abolishing Governmental Immunity," 1964 Duke L.J. 888.
2. The discussion in the text assumes that the legislature has not chosen to begin the constitutional amendment process to "reverse" an unpopular decision. If that were the case, the legislature would be participating in a constituent process which transcends ordinary legislative boundaries in the separation of powers model.
3. Of course, complete separation of powers does not exist in American state government any more than it does at the national level. While there may be complete separation of personnel, there is at least a partial sharing of function. Still, each branch may be said to be primarily responsible for its own respective function —with only limited interference from the other branches being contemplated.
4. They could, of course, develop such a policy over time by overturning judgments with an insufficient award and returning them to the trial courts for a rehearing on the issue of damages, but this would require a radical departure from the traditional division of labor between court and jury and further would be a process involving at least several years of decisions to sketch the judicially approved boundaries on the amount of awards.
5. See the discussion of United States v. Classic (1941) and Screws v. United States (1944) in Chapter 5.
6. For a discussion of the issue of deterrence, see the material in Chapter 4.
7. Because of the entity liability provisions, discussed later in this chapter, which make possible collectable judgments far in excess of the $250 maximum for individual-officer liability, the victim-plaintiff's recovery is not limited by these provisions.
8. See the discussion of the Tenney and Pierson cases in Chapter 2.
9. For the extent of officer liability see Sections 2.-1–2.09, above, and 5.04(b), below.
10. Note that the officer enforcing the statute in good faith escapes liability under the provisions of Section 2.07. Discriminatory application of an otherwise valid legislative enactment is specifically excluded from Section 4.03 to prevent constitutional deprivations, particularly of Fourteenth Amendment equal protection rights, so inflicted from securing the protection afforded by the section in question. Like-

wise, such enforcement patterns would fall outside the "good faith" officer defense in Section 2.07.

11. The types of damages permitted under the Act and their limitations will be discussed in the text accompanying Sections 5.01–5.06, below.

12. See Sections 14.01–14.03, below.

13. This is the only situation under the Act in which attorney's fees are considered part of the damage award. This is because the criminal or civil proceedings in question did not arise under the Act and therefore were not subject to the special provisions for attorney's fees which are set forth in Section 9, below.

14. See, for example, the cases cited in Hines, "Municipal Liability for Exemplary Damages," 16 Clev.-Mar. L. Rev. 304 (1966).

15. This might not be true, of course, if the entity maintains a consistent policy of depriving citizens of their constitutional rights, but in that case perhaps a serious blow to the entity is in order.

16. For a comment on the ordinary rule, see Note, "Liability of a State for Interest on a Judgment," 74 Dickinson L. Rev. 150 (1959).

17. Expunging of records is not entirely novel when those records have been made as the result of a constitutional deprivation. See the United States District Court's order to expunge school records relating to the explusion of students who were involved in constitutionally protected activity in Black Students of North Fort Myers Jr.-Sr. High School ex rel. Shoemaker v. Williams (M.D. Fla. 1970), a case brought under the provisions of 42 U.S.C. Section 1983.

18. This is not to overlook the possibility (indeed the probability) that some cases would be taken out of a public service orientation by these lawyers, but such actions, commendable as they are, provide no substitute for generally available well-qualified counsel.

19. It is assumed that over time the supply would rise to meet the demand for top-flight plaintiff's attorneys in constitutional deprivation damage suits if the economic rewards were suitable.

20. Query whether this "bargain" is ever more than a bargain in name only. In most instances it can be assumed that lawyers will have a relatively similar rate for similar cases, and the "buyer" is coming into a fairly restrained market.

21. Wright, *The Federal Tort Claims Act* 138 (1957).

22. Ibid. See also, Jayson, *Handling Federal Tort Claims* (1964), section 307.03 and the sources there cited.

23. This statement applies only to compensatory damages. In those limited cases under the Act where punitive damages are to be allowed under the plan it is not of the same force.

24. For our purposes here, we will assume that the state will bear the entire burden of the fees rather than there being a fee-sharing arrangement between the officer and the entity.

25. Possibly in some ideal world where the entity would be possessed of unlimited financial resources (hopefully derived from some source other than the taxation of its citizens) and the courts would be free from the problems of crowded dockets, it would be well to encourage every test case—no matter how frivolous—in an effort to ensure that no meritorious claim would be lost by lack of prosecution, but our present state of affairs is so far removed from this hypothetical world as to make it a matter of purest fantasy rather than realistic hope for the foreseeable future.

26. One could argue that the state has sufficient general interest in securing justice and preserving constitutional rights to pay a large fee even in cases involving only small awards, but it is highly unlikely that a legislature would accept the payment of fees ranging into the thousands of dollars for minimal judgments.

27. Also, artifically low limits on attorney's fees might be a subtle way to discourage suits under a supposedly liberal statute.

28. A third alternative, adopted by some states in the area of tort liability, is an

administrative body, but this alternative is inappropriate for the determination of matters of constitutional rights—this function in the United States having been vested in the judiciary.

29.    Hink and Schutter, "Some Thoughts on the American Law of Governmental Tort Liability," 20 Rutgers L. Rev. 710 (1966).

30.    See Section 15.01, which makes the statutory remedies in the Act exclusive and bars common law actions after the institution of suit under the Act. The same section also bars suits under the Act after common law actions have been instituted.

31.    The state statute could not bar an attempted recovery against the officer in federal court under 42 U.S.C. Section 1983 subsequent to institution of an action under the proposed Act.

32.    See Greenhill, "Should Governmental Immunity for Torts Be Re-examined, and, If So, by Whom?" 31 Texas Bar J. 1036, 1069 (1968) in which Mr. Justice Greenhill of the Texas Supreme Court recounts that representatives of the State Police and Firemen's Association had recommended abolition or modification of governmental immunity for their own protection after finding insurance for themselves expensive and difficult to obtain.

33.    See Kramer, "The Governmental Tort Immunity Doctrine in the United States 1790-1955," 1966 U. Ill. L.F. 795.

# TABLE OF CASES

# INDEX